RAW-
VITALIZE

RAW-VITALIZE

The Easy, 21-Day Raw Food Recharge

Mimi Kirk & Mia Kirk White

PHOTOGRAPHS BY MIKE MENDELL

THE COUNTRYMAN PRESS
A division of W. W. Norton & Company
Independent Publishers Since 1923

THIS BOOK IS DEDICATED TO THOSE WHO NEED A LITTLE
ENCOURAGEMENT TO TAKE BETTER CARE OF THEMSELVES

For information about special discounts for bulk purchases, please contact
W. W. Norton Special Sales at specialsales@wwnorton.com or 800-233-4830

Manufacturing by LSC Crawfordsville
Book design by Nick Caruso Design
Illustrations by Carolyn Kelly
Production manager: Devon Zahn

The Countryman Press
www.countrymanpress.com

A division of W. W. Norton & Company
500 Fifth Avenue, New York, NY 10110
www.wwnorton.com

978-1-68268-028-5 (pbk.)

10 9 8 7 6 5 4 3 2 1

CONTENTS

FOREWORDS   6

• • •

PART ONE •••• THE BASICS

RAW-VITALIZE TO REVITALIZE   12

YOU CAN DO IT   21

GET READY   30

DAILY DETAILS   36

PART TWO •••• THE 21-DAY PLAN

WEEK ONE   42
SHOPPING LIST   43

WEEK TWO   44
SHOPPING LIST   45

WEEK THREE   46
SHOPPING LIST   47

PART THREE •••• THE RECIPES

BREAKFAST   50

LUNCH   80

DINNER   132

ON-THE-GO SIMPLE SMOOTHIES   182

SNACKS   190

GUILT-FREE DESSERTS   202

• • •

AFTERWORD   219

ACKNOWLEDGMENTS   220

INDEX   221

FOREWORDS

MIMI KIRK

I was born in 1938. I'm the mother of four children and the grandmother of seven. At the age of seventy, I became a public figure when I was voted The Sexiest Vegetarian Over 50 in a nationwide contest conducted by PETA (People for the Ethical Treatment of Animals). This led to my first book deal, for *Live Raw*, and I've since written three more (including this one).

I've been a vegetarian/vegan for the better part of forty years. In my mid sixties, I met my current boyfriend and started cooking what he liked to eat, which was the standard American diet. Since we ate together, it made sense when I joined him in some of the foods. The next thing I knew, I had put on twenty-two pounds and did not feel as well as I was used to feeling. An annual physical check up confirmed my blood pressure and cholesterol were high. To make matters worse, for several months I had arthritic pains in my joints. When my doctor informed me it was age related and handed me a prescription, I was aghast. My family's health history included cancer, heart failure, strokes, diabetes, leukemia, and Parkinson's. They were all on prescription medications—handfuls, it seemed to me. I didn't want to follow in those footsteps. That was a wake-up call.

I wondered if it was, as the doctor said, age related, and if there truly was nothing I could do about it beyond fill the prescription. Something told me not to start taking anything until I could find a better way to cure myself. I left my doctor's office and without delay started researching whether natural approaches could cure what ailed me. Article after article showed that a plant-based diet of raw food could cure many different illnesses and diseases. I was used to eating a plant-based diet most of my life, but raw? On one hand I was happy to discover raw food cures, but on the other, I wasn't so happy. I'd always considered myself a lover of food and a good cook to boot, and the prospect of eating carrot sticks and celery did not appeal to me. In those early days, the raw food lifestyle seemed to still be in its infancy, but as I learned through these articles, raw food options had been around for many years. My research convinced me to give raw food a try. I thought there might be a way to continue my love of eating delicious foods while on a healing raw food diet.

I called my youngest daughter, Mia, hoping she would come along on the ride for moral support. The timing could not have been better for her, so together we embarked on a raw food journey. We decided to juice and eat raw food for a couple of weeks and see how we felt. To be honest, many of the online recipes I found didn't live up to my taste bud standards. A little disappointed, I started to adapt traditional cooked foods I loved into raw food recipes. This was when I realized how delicious raw food could be. I was mesmerized. Thinly sliced zucchini emerged as lasagna noodles. Sundried and heirloom tomatoes, blended with herbs and spices, metamorphosed into a delicious uncooked red sauce. Basil pesto was creamy goodness even without the cheese. Fermented cashew nuts gave the zucchini lasagna a cheesy taste. I can honestly say food never tasted so good. I felt I was onto some futuristic way of eating. The food was tasty and, best of all, I started to feel more energetic. I thought I looked a little younger as well. Mia told me she was having the same results. After eating raw vegan for two weeks, I decided to make this my lifestyle. I was feeling good and creating some good food in the process. Six months later, my doctor's visit confirmed my choice: my blood pressure and cholesterol were normal and my arthritic pain was nonexistent.

Since then, I've written *Live Raw, Live Raw Around the World,* and *The Ultimate Book of Modern Juicing.* I trained to be a raw food plant-based chef at Matthew Kenny's Culinary Academy. I'm an internationally known speaker, coach, and consultant, and I teach raw food preparation classes. In addition to my many speaking engagements, I have a YouTube channel where I show my audience how to prepare raw food dishes, and it has been viewed by millions. I specialize in adapting traditionally cooked dishes into easy raw vegan meals. I hope this book, which I co-wrote with Mia when we recently needed a recharge, will help you to try the raw food lifestyle.

MIA KIRK WHITE

At the age of twelve, I was diagnosed with juvenile arthritis. This, along with growing up in a vegetarian household, started my interest in nutritional healing and bodywork. When my mother called me and suggested we try a raw food diet together, I was happy to start down this road. Now I consider myself a raw food chef and teach classes on healing with whole foods. I believe in the innate healing power of the body through whole foods and positive thinking.

Like most women attempting to balance family and work, I spent numerous years struggling with my weight. At one point in my life, I had clothes sizes 8 through 16 in my closet. I tried every diet on the market, losing a few pounds and then gaining them back as soon as I stopped starving myself. I was on an emotional weight rollercoaster and I feared I would never get off. I realized that every time I made unhealthy dietary choices, my arthritis would act up. My joints stiffened, my stomach bloated, and my overall energy was low. I thought I lost my inner glow.

When I changed my diet to include more raw food, I felt so much better. But it was hard to stick to that. It occurred to me that the times I made unhealthy choices were also the times I wasn't organized with my meals. My busy weekly schedule consists of taking care of a demanding business and being intricately involved in my children's after school and weekend activities. So when I can organize my meals each week, it's much easier for me to eat healthy, which is why this plan is so great. Most of my friends have busy lives as well, which constantly reminds me how important it is for us to feel our best so we can better support our lifestyle demands. When I got off track after eating cooked vegan foods, it was an indication for me that eating raw made me healthier and more energetic. This is one of the main reasons my mom and I decided to share Raw-Vitalize. Our experiences could benefit others who wish to change their lifestyles, which will get them on their way to looking and feeling fantastic!

when you only accept what you want, you will always get what you want.

1

THE BASICS

RAW-VITALIZE TO REVITALIZE

How Raw-Vitalize Started

We are believers in Hippocrates' quote, "Let food be thy medicine and medicine be thy food." There is power in food. The right foods can heal us and the wrong foods can make us sick. We have a choice to be conscious at each meal, whether to feed our cells and our immune system or to deplete them. We can eat for good health and at the same time enjoy the mouthwatering flavors that fresh, plant-based foods offer us.

We've both worked with many clients over the years, helping them to enjoy a healthier lifestyle and prevent looming diseases while teaching them to prepare raw food. We've tailored plans to fit each individual's busy schedule and special needs. On one of our daily phone calls, we were discussing how satisfying it was that our clients achieved such great results and felt renewed, invigorated, less stressed, and more energetic after working with us. A lightbulb went off that this information could be valuable for a larger audience in need of a health improvement. We didn't start out to write a book—we did this for our clients and our own health—but when we realized the positive results that were possible, we decided a book was in order. We pooled our ideas and experiences and got to work.

We live in different cities and, after many months, hundreds of hours, many phone calls, dozens of Facetime and Skype meetings, a rendezvous in Spain, another in

California, and several personal 21-day test runs, we knew we had a great working plan. Our awareness renewed, we knew exactly what worked and how to make it simple.

What to Expect

We don't believe diets work so please don't consider this a diet. Losing weight should not be your objective—being healthy should. This 21-day plan is not a quick detox or cleanse. This style of eating will rekindle your health and wellbeing, and will start you on a radiant path for the rest of your life. If you've been eating fast food and processed foods, then this plan—in some ways—might feel like a cleanse but you will never be hungry or feel you are going without anything.

We created a collection of simple recipes, which are colorful, beautiful to look at, and easy to prepare. They are nourishing, satisfying, and will fuel you throughout your busy day. Our flavorful recipes include simple techniques, handy tips, and no-fuss shopping. Most of the recipes can be made in approximately 10 to 15 minutes, making it easy to keep your 21-day commitment and beyond.

Q:

Will I be hungry?

A:

Raw food is not just celery and carrot sticks—it is far more than crudités. Raw foods are balanced, tasty, and satisfying meals. In fact, you might be too full to eat all the food we scheduled for each day. We don't think you will be hungry after a meal, but if you are, you can find delicious, quick-and-easy treats in our Snacks chapter.

Since texture affects our enjoyment of food as much as flavor, our recipes include a variety of juicy, creamy, and crunchy foods to keep you scrumptiously satisfied. We promise you won't be bored. Some of these recipes might become your new comfort food when you are stressed or not feeling your best, given that they are full of nutrients and supply an immediate boost of energy.

Our meals are simple and luscious, and minimal equipment is needed. Organization is the key to success and we've organized your pantry staples and weekly shopping lists, which will take the pressure off what you need for supplies. While fixing family meals, it might be tempting to just eat what you are making them rather than prepare another meal for yourself. The trick is to prepare your tempting meal first so you have something to look forward to eating while you are cooking something else for your family. You might be surprised that your family will want to try out these enticing meals as well. All your meals will be light, filling, and quick to prepare. We combined our kitchen tricks to ensure that snacking on the wrong foods is a thing of the past. Your metabolism will be balanced with the proper flow of meals, which will also supply the right amount of nutrients and vitamins for your body's daily needs.

We think the easiest way to follow the 21-day recharge is as written; however, it is not inflexible. Life should not be so rigid. If you don't feel like fixing a particular meal on that specific day, the plan allows you to mix and match foods, choose alternatives, or replace a meal with a creamy smoothie or a snack. You are also welcome to repeat your favorite meals.

We were encouraged to come up with quick recipes for those times when you just want to crawl into bed without preparing anything but still want something to eat. These quick-to-make meals, smoothies, snacks, and desserts are tempting luxury indulgences to make this 21-day recharge as easy as possible.

Q:

Do I have to eat only raw foods?

A:

During the 21 days we suggest only raw foods, but after you complete the 21 days you might decide to continue eating all raw or you might decide 50 to 70 percent raw is right for you. Whatever you decide, this experience will allow you to kick off a new healthy way of eating.

What is a Raw Food Lifestyle?

You know by reading current magazines and shopping the health section at your local bookstore that there is proof that healthy eating gives you more energy. It can also make you more productive and increase your brain function. Fresh, live foods make you feel and look amazing. Raw foods will help you sail through the day and still have endless energy after work. No more running on empty. The best part is you don't need professional qualifications to make raw food. It's the easiest food to prepare on the planet. You can't burn yourself on the oven or a hot pot. You don't need to wear those strange-looking oven mitts that make you look like you have a right and left thumb. Best of all, you won't have to scrub pots and pans and baked-on food stuck to the Pyrex dish.

We assume you already know how to cook. Easy right? You take out a frying pan, drizzle in some oil, and toss in some chopped veggies and onions, sauté until al dente, and that's it. You may even fire up the grill. But it is a little different with raw food. No heat is required or desired. How do we bring flavor to our food, you might wonder? The natural, fresh taste of the vegetable or fruit is the star. Food tastes exactly how it grew straight from the garden or farm. We give it the slightest bit of help from naturally delicious spices and herbs, seeds, and berries. That—plus a few other tricks up our sleeves—is how raw food is transformed into something extraordinary and worth devouring.

Q:

Is all the food cold?

A:

It's a misconception that all raw food is cold. You will be able to enjoy some warmed foods including soups, vegetable pastas, and drinks. All of these can be warmed and still be in keeping with not heating anything over 115 to 118 degrees. In cold weather, spices are a good way to warm up a recipe. A pinch of chili, cinnamon, or ginger goes a long way in warming our bodies.

There is pleasure and health to be gained in the kitchen and with simple, good-quality ingredients we hope to show you how it's done! Food is not just about fuel or eating and if the saying is true—that time is short and we should live every moment—then preparing the food should be just as delightful as eating it. Large amounts of money are spent making kitchens beautiful and yet there is so much concern about the time it takes to prepare a meal. This suggests that the kitchen is a place to spend as little time as possible. With our quick meals, we are not trying to rush you out of the kitchen; rather, we want to give those who are busy a way to enjoy making appetizing meals and maybe even enjoy the kitchen again. Why waste time in life making the things we do a chore? Let's begin living our journey every moment, with pleasure wherever we are and whatever we're doing. Whether large or small, a kitchen is a beautiful place to let your creativity, love, and joy bloom.

Raw food has become increasingly refined since it first became popular. Preparing raw food has fascinated us for years, but now it has become a global phenomenon. These ideas have penetrated the restaurant scene with raw food eateries popping up all over the world. One reason raw food has become popular is it has natural anti-aging effects. It has also gained popularity for reversing and preventing many diseases. Raw food can make you feel good physically, mentally, and spiritually. Hollywood celebrities and athletes have adopted a raw vegan lifestyle for physical appearance, endurance, and overall ultimate health. Raw food is alkaline-forming, and rich with vitamins and minerals needed to heal our bodies and keep them at peak performance.

Another reason is that this lifestyle includes such a variety of fresh, healthy, simple, real food—it would make any gourmet table groan with abundance—which is far from the notion some may have that raw food is solely celery and carrot sticks. Aside from being tasty and gorgeous on the eyes, raw food can keep our digestive system healthy. Raw food is recognized for its enzymes and high-nutrient content. When food is heated over 115 degrees, it is known to destroy certain vitamins and nutrients. Heat also destroys the enzymes. It's true, our bodies naturally produce enzymes, but as we age, our natural enzyme production begins to dramatically decrease. Some raw food experts, including David Wolfe, Dr. Robert O. Young, and Dr. Gabriel Cousens, claim that enzyme-dead cooked foods place a burden on our organs and pancreas. This burden exhausts the organs as they become overworked. We need enzymes for proper digestion and gut health. A raw food lifestyle provides these enzymes. Eating raw, plant-based foods have been known to prevent and cure many diseases including certain cancers. Raw food is now mentioned in several health documentaries as an important healing modality.

In keeping with the theme of this book—to make meals simple, easy, and satisfying—we have not included dehydrated raw foods. When you get deeply into eating raw, it becomes fun to make breads, crackers, cookies, and other dehydrated items. We also make nut cheeses that take time to ferment and age. We have intentionally left out any time-consuming recipes. The artistic world of raw food has developed many gourmet dishes. Today, you can find raw food culinary schools and academies where you can learn to make plant-based food at its best. But for now, we want to make things easy for you. We will teach you how to quickly turn beautiful produce into gorgeously tasty meals, while at the same time improving your health and wellbeing.

Is Raw-Vitalize for You?

Raw-Vitalize is for anyone who wants to restore, rejuvenate, and revitalize their health. It's for anyone who would like a lifestyle adjustment and for those who want a great collection of time-saving, deliciously healthy recipes.

- Have you ever set a personal goal to eat healthier and either didn't stick with it very long or maybe never started at all?
- Have you ever been raw food curious?
- Have you tried raw food but didn't feel it was right for you?
- Do you think eating raw food is just too confusing and time consuming?
- Have you entertained a raw food lifestyle, but somehow got off track?
- Are you looking for ways to improve your health, both physically and mentally?
- Are you ready to recharge and rejuvenate you life?
- Would you like to have access to simple, quick, mouthwatering, healthy recipes?

If any of these scenarios fit you, we've got you covered. You might feel you're too busy right now to change your way of eating. We know how difficult change can be, especially if you have a full-time job, are a parent, or can't stop long enough in a day to catch your breath. Some days you might be so busy you feel lucky if you have enough time to grab a quick lunch or just get dinner on the table. You might wonder why you should bother to change. Ask yourself these simple questions:

- How long can my body take stress?
- How long can my body go without proper nutrients?
- How long can I feel tired and lack energy before it causes me to get sick?
- How long can I run on empty?

The simple answer is your body will feel the effects of neglect and bad eating faster than you can imagine. Stress plays havoc on your immune system and adrenals. Waiting until you get sick or exhausted might change your life and dash your dreams. We are professional working women with families—we understand, and we are here to help you. We tried and tested Raw-Vitalize many times over and figured out the easiest way for you to enjoy raw food for 21 days and get the proper nutrients your body needs. We honestly feel this way of eating will improve your life in a variety of ways. It's easy, enjoyable, and doable. It works!

Q:

How many servings are in a recipe?

A:

All the recipes are intended for one person. If you are preparing recipes for more than one you can double or triple the recipes. The exceptions are desserts, which will make a few servings as they are refrigerated or frozen for convenience. Make a dessert once and eat it several times during the 21 days.

Remember how fast last year went by and how quickly the days or a month seem to pass. Well, just think about how fast 21 days will fly by and, by the end of it, you will have made major changes to better your health along with feeling reenergized and positive. You might prevent some looming health issues, or a current illness may even disappear. One thing for sure is you will be on the right path to improve your health, longevity, and happiness.

Accountability could be a key to your success. See if you can enlist a family member or friend to do the 21-day recharge with you. It's good to have a pal to help keep you motivated.

life can be simple when you decide that it will be.

WHAT IS INCLUDED IN RAW-VITALIZE?

- One hundred delicious, easy-to-follow raw food recipes including juices, breakfasts, lunches, dinners, snacks, and desserts.
- Weekly organized shopping lists, which will save you time and money, and make your life easier.
- A week-at-a-glance menu plan, which allows you to mix and match meals, or just follow the plan as written.
- A pantry staples list so you will have all your dry goods on hand.
- Loads of helpful timesaving ideas, including how to make and prep ingredients for your weekday smoothie or juice in advance.
- Inspirational and encouraging messages to keep you motivated.
- Hydrating water ideas and beautiful ice cubes.
- A few exercise ideas you can easily incorporate into your busy day.

YOU CAN DO IT

Real Life

The truth is we all weaken at times when it comes to food by making poor choices. We put off regular exercise because we feel lazy, make excuses, or find restraints placed on our time. But what's at stake if we weaken to harmful food temptations too many times or avoid daily exercise? The answer is our immune system gets run down and we get sick! If we want to thrive and not just survive we have to make a few changes. To be healthier we must not consume processed and chemical-laden foods. We must exercise, practice low alcohol consumption, and avoid smoking. All these suggestions will add good years to our lives. Blowing out candles on our one hundredth birthday is a great thought, but we want good health right now at any age—and Raw-Vitalize can help to supercharge our lives.

Here are some motivating factors and benefits you will gain when you make some dietary changes, exercise daily, and think positive thoughts.

- You can avoid disease, pain, and suffering.
- You can have more energy and feel stronger.
- You can enjoy better mental clarity.
- You can improve your mood and have less stress.
- You can have more radiant skin.
- You can lose extra, unwanted fat.

- You can enjoy better sleep.
- You can fight off infections and inflammation.
- You can look and feel younger.
- You can enjoy life more.
- You can have more time to spend with loved ones.
- You can have time to accomplish and live your dream.
- You can feel more confident and empowered.
- You can spend your money on something you want rather than on pharmaceuticals.
- You can live longer and happier.

For Busy People

Even if you enjoy cooking, there are times at the end of a long day when you are just not in the mood to spend hours in the kitchen fixing dinner. Picking up fast food on your way home from work might be the quickest choice but maybe not the healthiest one. In contrast, what if you could fix a gratifying, healthy meal in 10 to 15 minutes and all the ingredients were already in your kitchen? Do you think you could kick off your shoes, put on something comfortable, and make a quick and nourishing dinner? This is the exact reason we created simple dishes. Step-by-step instructions and easy-to-follow, fresh, creative recipes will help you keep a promise you once made to take better care of yourself. Raw food does not have to be complicated. Our friendly, approachable recipes are for those who love to cook and those who don't. Shopping and planning can be one of the most stressful parts of preparing a meal and the good news is we've done the work for you. With our weekly shopping lists, kitchen essentials, and raw food pantry staples list, you will be sure to have all the ingredients on hand necessary to make simple, great-tasting meals in minutes.

We live in a busy world and even though we want to take care of our health by exercising and eating right, sometimes it seems like just too much work to sit down and figure out what we are going to eat for the day—let alone for a full week. When we haven't planned what we are going to eat, we leave ourselves open to grabbing junk food because there is no healthy food option when we become hungry. Even a protein bar could be loaded with sugar, and that cup of coffee can backfire by putting more stress on our adrenals. Quick meal replacement drinks will not bring lasting health. We say eat real food! Cut out processed foods made with ingredients you can't pronounce and which are thought to be responsible for obesity and disease. To have ultimate health, we must eat unprocessed fresh foods. Don't wait until you have to reverse a disease—eat the right foods and you can prevent many illnesses. If you are in a hurry and need to grab a bite, we have plenty of recipes for healthy snacks. Nobody really likes to prepare two different meals, one for family and one for yourself, but because our meals are so quick to prepare, you will not mind fixing your meal first so it's waiting for you while you prepare your family's meal. By doing this, you will not be tempted to break your 21-day commitment. Of course, it would be ideal if your family was willing to eat these delicious meals as well—we suggest you give it a try.

Q:

Can I eat out while on the plan?

A:

Yes—we find most restaurants will adjust a meal to fit your needs. Remember to just stay raw. Salads are the best place to start. You can ask the server to leave off the chicken and replace it with avocado. You can request a dinner-size salad instead of a side salad. You can ask the server to see if the cook/chef will fix you a plate of all-raw vegetables—any fresh vegetables they have in the kitchen will be perfect. In Italy, this crudités platter is properly called *pinzimonio*. A large platter with chunks of cauliflower, broccoli, cucumber, and other in-season vegetables are served with a sharp knife, good olive oil, and sea salt. You will be satisfied eating out if you follow our advice and be mindful when ordering. You can always grab a raw snack or dessert at home if you still feel the need for something more to eat. The less uncomfortable you are when ordering in a restaurant, the better your family and friends will feel about what you are eating. More times than not, friends at our table say they wish they ordered what we had.

Busy people like to be effective and many times put their needs last. We will show you a few tricks to make your meals quick and easy. You are honestly going to feel happier taking a few extra minutes for yourself. Being healthy will help you be more productive and less stressed. Raw-Vitalize was designed for busy people with busy schedules. With invaluable, time-saving advice, appetizing recipes, pantry staples, and weekly shopping lists, a week-at-a-glance chart and our well-planned schedule, all you need to do is to make a 21-day commitment, follow the simple recipes, and you will achieve your desired results.

FIVE STEPS TO SUCCESS

1. If possible, purchase your complete pantry staples list and then shop once a week for your produce with the provided shopping list. This will allow you to have all the weekly foods necessary to make your meals.

2. Follow directions for the easy recipes. Some can be made ahead and others take 10 minutes to prepare.

3. If you don't feel like preparing one of the meals from the weekly chart, no problem. Swap in one of the easy five-minute recipes from the "Snacks" chapter, such as Zucchini Ribbons, or Cacao Banana Smoothie, and you will have an alternative satisfying meal in minutes.

4. If you are eating out with friends, we tell you how to make it easy and delicious and still stay raw.

5. We teach you how to organize your own space in the kitchen, making it easier to separate what you eat and what your family eats. This is your time and it's important for you take care of yourself.

That's all there is to it. We plan the week's menu for you, give you the shopping list, and, with just basic kitchen tools, your meal is ready in no time. And by the way, if you think chopping veggies looks like a chore after you get home from work, keep in mind that chopping and dicing can be a calming ritual and a great stress reliever.

Anyone can change their eating habits with the right tools and Raw-Vitalize is so simple to follow, it's the perfect tool for success. Keep in mind, this is not a detox, cleanse, diet, or temporary fix. Often the first few days of a detox can make you feel worse before you feel better; some people quit too early because they can't get by those first few days. With Raw-Vitalize, you will start feeling better right away. This can easily be used as a lifelong change even after you complete the 21 days. However you choose to use this plan, you will definitely be feeling better in no time and you will have some delicious recipes to use forever.

Q:

Is the plan difficult to maintain while cooking for others?

A:

Following our method will make it easy for you to stay on the plan even if you are cooking different food for family members. We recommend you prepare your food first before starting your family's meal. This will allow everyone to sit at the dinner table at the same time and enjoy a meal together. If your meal is already prepared before you cook theirs, you will not be temped to eat what you are fixing them, as your food will be even more enticing. This would be a good time to introduce your family to some Raw-Vitalize desserts.

Better Digestion

Many people have bad digestion and experience a feeling of fullness after eating and assume it's natural. Cooked foods have lost their enzymes so it makes sense that undigested food stays in your body for some time after a meal. When food is properly digested, it will not remain in the stomach very long. Raw foods can help build a healthy internal ecosystem if you follow a few suggestions. We highly recommend that you eat slowly and chew each mouthful thoroughly until it's completely broken down into liquid form. This is best accomplished when you eat mindfully and take smaller bites. Chewing is most important when eating cruciferous vegetables such as kale, collards, cabbage, broccoli, cauliflower, and Brussels sprouts, which may be harder to digest unless chewed well. When drinking a vegetable juice or smoothie, the fiber is broken down, which aids in digestion. If you find you have digestive issues, purchase digestive enzymes and take as directed before or directly after eating. We recommend purchasing fermented foods as well, such as kimchi, sauerkraut, or kombucha. Adding fermented foods to your daily diet will help to build a healthy internal system for quickly digesting food. Fermented foods have high nutritional value as well. A tablespoon a day of vegan fermented veggies or half a bottle of kombucha daily should be enough to get your digestion going. Fermented foods are easily made at home, but you can find delicious raw versions at a health food store or on the Internet for time convenient.

Practice Mindfulness

Mindful eating is an important part of health and wellness. When you sit down to a meal, be mindful of what is on your plate. Most times we start eating without even thinking. Look at what is on your plate for a few moments before starting to eat. Take a few deep breaths and relax your shoulders, body, and mind. Being in the moment when you eat will help you make better eating choices, chew consciously, eat less, and feel more satisfied. Eating when rushed causes stress eating and is one of the biggest contributors to overeating. When our body is in a state of stress, it produces an excess amount of cortisol, a hormone that can increase our appetite. Deep breathing will help you make better choices and help to relieve stress. This deep breathing method can be used any time you feel stress coming on during your day. By practicing this technique, you will strengthen your mindfulness and have better control over stress.

Add In Some Exercise

If you already exercise, keep it up. If you don't, we ask that you do something every day to improve your muscle tone and flexibility. Do any of the following—walking is one of the best overall physical exercises. Try to walk at least 30 minutes daily for 21 days. Increase the time a little each week. You may choose to do pushups for 21 days. It's okay to have your knees on the mat if you are new to working your upper body. Try to incorporate pushups or sit ups to help strengthen your cores. Increase the number of pushups and/or sit ups over the 21 days. If you sit at a desk most of the day, get up every half an hour and move around your office. Have some water, use the restroom, and do anything you can to get movement in on a daily basis. If you already have a workout schedule, be sure to continue during the 21 days and you'll notice your increased energy.

Stay Hydrated

It's very important to stay hydrated, so we found an easy way to drink more water. We love infused waters and ice cubes. Here are just a few of our favorites.

WATERS

Into a jar of filtered water add any of the following, seal with lid, and let sit in refrigerator until flavored;

INGREDIENTS

Cucumber and lemon

Celery

Basil

3 types of berries

Mint and lemon

Pineapple

Ginger and lemon

ICE CUBES

METHOD

Pour filtered water into the ice cube tray. Place a small slice of citrus and a blueberry or strawberry into the water. Freeze. Try mint, basil, or other herbs and fruits.

Keep a few mason jars of water in your refrigerator that are ready to grab and go. Drinking water is one of the most important daily habits to acquire. If you are not used to drinking water throughout the day, the ideas above will help you to drink more water. Health authorities recommend eight ounces eight times a day. If you wait until you are thirsty to drink, you are already dehydrated.

● ○ ○

*hydration is the word of the day.
drink lots of water.*

GET READY

Equipment

The basic equipment needed is a blender, food processor, sharp kitchen knife, and a cutting board.

Most things can be done with a good sharp knife and a cutting board. However, in the name of proper textures, a food processor is important. Food processor chopping can be done in seconds. A blender is another necessary item, which will help to make smoothies, dressings, and blended sauces. There are no dehydrated recipes, but if you happen to own one, then some foods can be warmed in the dehydrator. Alternatively, our soups and warm drinks can be warmed on a stove burner, but keep in mind the rule of never heating over 118 degrees. Body temperature is the desired outcome.

Pantry Staples

Certain ingredients pop up repeatedly in the recipes and once your cupboard is stocked with these essential items you will only need to add some fresh produce on a weekly basis. For your convenience, and if possible, purchase these ingredients all at once. If it's not possible to buy all your staples at one time, your shopping list will remind you that you need them for the week. Check your pantry to see if you already own some of these items. Most people will have the spices, oils, and other common items.

PANTRY STAPLES
INGREDIENTS FREQUENTLY USED FOR 21-PLUS DAYS

Four 16-ounce bags raw almonds

Four 16-ounce bags raw cashews

Two 16-ounce bags raw walnuts

8-ounce bag raw pecans

8-ounce bag raw pine nuts

7-ounce bag unsweetened coconut flakes

Two 16-ounce bags pumpkin seeds

Three 16-ounce bags raw sunflower seeds

8-ounce bag hemp seeds

16-ounce bag flaxseeds

12-ounce jar raw almond butter

8-ounce package chia seeds

16-ounce bag cacao powder

16-ounce bag gluten-free oats

8-ounce bag goji berries

8-ounce bag dried cranberries, cherries, or raisins

16-ounce container pure maple syrup or sweetener of choice (no white sugar)

Two 16-ounce containers Medjool dates

16 ounces sundried tomatoes, no oil

One 6-pack raw, untoasted Nori sheets

Dijon mustard

4 ounces capers

8 ounces black olives

8 ounces coconut oil

16-ounce bottle extra-virgin olive oil

5-ounce bottle sesame oil

8-ounce jar vegan mayo

8-ounce jar raw tahini

10-ounce bottle of gluten-free tamari

16-ounce bottle cider vinegar

16-ounce carton coconut milk

2 ounces dulse, whole leaf or flakes

4 ounces nutritional yeast

Black pepper

Cardamom powder

Chili flakes and chili powder

Cinnamon powder

Cumin powder

Curry powder

Garlic powder

Herbs de Provence

Italian seasonings

Onion powder

Paprika

Smoked paprika

Sea salt or pink Himalayan salt

Turmeric powder

Pure vanilla extract

One 16-ounce carton coconut water

1 box green tea

Filtered water

About Organic Produce

The quality of the food you purchase does make a difference in the way food tastes. We recommend you buy the best and freshest organic ingredients you can find and you will be more than halfway there to preparing an extraordinary meal. Real food with real ingredients beats manufactured, processed food in boxes, bags, and cans. We think it's very important to eat organic foods because pesticides and chemicals permeate conventional food and the crop soil depletes nutritional value. All this is changing our biology and

harming our cells, plus our planet's ecosystem. The perpetrators of genetically modified organisms (GMO) have never heard of the saying "Don't mess with Mother Nature." Foods today—especially if they are altered—do not have the vitamin content they had years ago. Pesticides are causing chronic diseases and early aging. We need now—more than ever—to be responsible for what foods we purchase and put in our bodies. We know not everyone can find or afford organic produce at their supermarkets or farmers' markets, but try to buy as local and fresh as possible. Many farmers are not certified organic, but they are currently not spraying their food. It takes years to convert to organic and, since certification can be costly, some farmers choose not to apply for certification. Know your grower at farmers' markets and they will tell you how they grow their produce. That being said, below are a few items you must always buy organic as they hold the highest amount of pesticides. When it comes to inorganic, strawberries are the worst. We know—no one is ever happy to hear this, but strawberries decorate many buffet or party tables and those little pores hold more pesticides than other fruits and vegetables. Other highly pesticide-laden foods to avoid (unless organic) are apples, nectarines, peaches, celery, grapes, spinach, lettuce, cherries, tomatoes, cherry tomatoes, bell peppers, and cucumbers. Foods that are okay if they are not organic include avocados, pineapple, cabbage, sweet peas, onions, asparagus, mangos, papayas, kiwis, eggplant, honeydew, grapefruit, cantaloupe, and cauliflower. Do your best to buy all organic, especially when juicing. You can find frozen organic fruits in most health food stores. They are well worth buying if you can't buy fresh organic as they retain their vitamins when flash frozen. We recommend not purchasing foods from China, as their organic food safety standards may be different than ours, and many reports find non-food fillers in several items. It is best to avoid any food from China at this time.

Full Disclosure of Products Used

While "Just stay raw" is our motto, many raw cooks use an ingredient or two that is not raw. We chose to use some of these ingredients in our recipes as well since we feel they contain vitamins and minerals that compensate for not being raw. Full disclosures for ingredients that are not raw include maple syrup, nutritional yeast, tamari, regular cut gluten-free oats, Dijon mustard, and vegan mayonnaise. You can purchase gluten-free oats online or soak oat groats—which are raw—overnight in warm water. Nutritional yeast and maple syrup contain enough flavor, vitamins, and mineral to make it worth the choice. Maple syrup is high in minerals, but can be replaced with coconut nectar or granules, yacón syrup, or date paste—and, in some cases, stevia. Nutritional yeast gives a cheesy taste and is loaded with B vitamins and 18 amino acids. We do not have a substitute for nutritional yeast, so eliminate it from the recipe if you choose not to use it. We mention Dijon mustard in a couple of recipes; if you care not to use it, try mustard powder or mustard seeds to make your own mustard replacement. Cashews make a great mayo (see page 111 for a recipe), but if you prefer not to make your own mustard and mayo from scratch (or don't have the time), store-bought mustard and vegan mayo might be the best time-saving choice for you. Tamari is traditionally a liquid byproduct made during the fermentation of miso and has an abundance of amino acids derived from fermented soy protein. It aids in the digestion of fruits and vegetables while being rich in several minerals. It is a good source of vitamin B3, protein, manganese, and tryptophan. We find the taste much better than other similar products on the market; however, coconut amino can be a good replacement.

If you have nut allergies, try replacing some of the recipes containing nuts with seeds.

Helpful Tips

During the 21 days, keep your blender and food processor on the countertop for quick access. If you have an immersion blender, they are good for small-batch dressings. If you don't have time to clean your appliance in the morning, put soapy water in your blender or food processor after use for easy cleanup when you return home.

You don't need years of culinary training to know your own taste preferences. We encourage you to use your own senses of smell, sight, and taste with every recipe. You may like more or less garlic, more or less salt and pepper, or more or less sweetener. If you don't like a spice or vegetable, replace it with one you prefer. Feel free to adjust any and all ingredients to your liking. Plate your food so it's beautiful to look at, as it will be served to a special someone—that someone is you! We think plating is important. If it looks good, there's a great chance your mind will signal your palate.

If you choose not to make your own almond milk, you can purchase it at a super-market. Please check the ingredients on the carton, though, and be sure to buy a brand without sugar. We think homemade tastes far better and is not processed, making it much healthier. However, we understand time constraints, so do what is easiest for you. Once you try homemade almond milk, you will see how simple and quick it is to make and how rich and creamy it tastes.

Don't let the amount of ingredients in a recipe put you off, as a closer look will reveal many of the ingredients are herbs and spices, which contribute to rich flavors and the nutritional value of a recipe. Various ingredients will be chopped with a food processor or blender, allowing the machine to do the work for you. We promise you the 10 or 15 minutes it takes for you to prepare a meal will be well worth it in terms of health benefits and scrumptious food.

If you find a favorite salad dressing recipe in the book, double up when making it and use it on other salads. While chopping veggies, you might want to chop some extra for the next day's recipe and seal them in an airtight glass jar to save time. Don't keep chopped veggies for more than one to two days, as vitamins may be lost.

You will notice that some of the same ingredients are used in several recipes, which will save you time and money at the market. One recipe might call for one-quarter piece of red bell pepper and another recipe that week or the next might call for half of a red bell pepper. So in this way you will be using the majority of food on your weekly shopping list. Some leftover ingredients can be saved for the following week. To keep greens and veggies fresh, wrap them in paper towels, place them in a plastic bag, and refrigerate. Before shopping for the following week, check your leftover vegetables and fruits so you don't have to duplicate what you already have.

Not all raw foods are eaten cold. Food and drink can be lightly warmed on a stovetop and still maintain their enzymes. Warm as much as you might a baby bottle: warm to the touch but not hot. Food can be eaten at room temperature instead of directly from the refrigerator. During cold months, add warming spices such as garlic, ginger, chili, cinnamon, and cayenne. Warm your plate or bowl before plating to give a feeling of warmth to your food.

Soaking Information

In preparing some of the recipes, nuts, seeds, and sundried tomatoes need to soak, which take what we call passive time, meaning you are not involved in the process. Soaking in water while you are away from home or overnight while you are sleeping doesn't take any time away from your schedule. All you need to do is place nuts in a bowl and cover them with filtered water and voilà—now they do the work by themselves. Recipes take around 10 to 15 minutes to prepare, not including soaking time or removing ingredients from the cupboard or refrigerator.

When nuts and seeds are soaked, they neutralize the enzyme inhibitors and aid the production of beneficial enzymes, enabling better digestion. It might be a time saver to check the weekly recipe and soak all of one kind of nut for three days' use. After soaking, nuts can be rinsed well, drained, and stored in a jar with a tight-fitting lid. Store in the refrigerator for a maximum of three days and rinse well before using. In a pinch, if you don't use the nuts in three days, you can freeze them for a later use.

Organizing your kitchen is very important. Clean out one cupboard in your kitchen for your raw staple ingredients. If you don't have an extra cupboard, purchase a large plastic tub to keep your ingredients in. Quick access means you will know exactly where everything is to make preparing your meals more efficient.

Rule of thumb when preparing meals: Put all the ingredients listed in the recipe on the kitchen counter or at your workstation before starting to prepare the meal. The French culinary phrase for this is called *mise en place*, which means putting in place. This method is used in professional and home kitchens alike to refer to organizing and arranging all the required ingredients for a dish prior to preparation..

DAILY DETAILS

Something to consider is how much food is right for you. Breakfast can be filling and there might not be any stomach room for a smoothie until mid-morning or late afternoon. If that is the case, then use your own judgment and listen to your body. Getting enough nutrients to keep you energized is important, so it would be better to eat smaller meals more times a day to keep your metabolism steady. Each person is different when it comes to what the right amount of food should be. You will be clear on this subject a few days into the recharge.

Measurements for each recipe are designed for one person, but if you choose to eat less, then eat what works best for you. If there is too little food, feel free to add more or have a raw snack. Eating three meals a day plus snacks helps to keep your metabolism balanced, so try not to miss meals. If your family is eating raw with you, double or triple the recipe. We know from many testing experiences that the whole family enjoys these meals, with desserts being especially favored.

AWAKEN We recommend this as a daily ritual. Drink it on an empty stomach. This hydrating drink is full of vitamins and will alkalize your body by removing toxins. It will boost your immune system, neutralize free radicals, reduce bloating, improve digestion, and make your skin glow. Wait 30 minutes before consuming solid food. A good rule of thumb is to drink this elixir immediately upon awakening before you shower or get dressed. This will allow the 30 minutes you need before breakfast or a smoothie.

AWAKEN

INGREDIENTS

8 or more ounces filtered water

Juice of ½ lemon

1 teaspoon cider vinegar

Cayenne, to taste

1 teaspoon maple syrup or sweetener of choice (no white sugar)
(optional—once you get used to the taste, no sweetener is necessary)

METHOD

Put all the ingredients into a glass and stir to combine. Alternatively, place in a jar with a tight-fitting lid and shake vigorously.

SMOOTHIES We recommend a daily smoothie to keep you satisfied throughout the day. Smoothies give you energy and bring clarity. If you prefer, you can swap a smoothie for a breakfast any day you like or drink it as an afternoon snack. Your brain will thank you. (See On-the-Go Simple Smoothies, pages 182–89)

BREAKFAST is an important daily ritual. It can set the tone for how you will take care of yourself for the rest of the day. We need to feed our cells so as not to deplete our energy. Breakfast jump-starts our metabolism and keeps energy high and balanced all day. You can have a smoothie for breakfast, or the breakfast recipe we recommend. You can also eat any mono fruit you like in the morning, which means choose one fruit and eat as much as you like.

LUNCH re-energizes your body in the middle of the day and helps with focus and concentration. Lunch is also important to keep your metabolism active and help you feel energized through the balance of your day. We understand it's not always easy to take time for a proper lunch. If you reach for a conventional protein bar or a coffee drink, it will have you in a slump an hour or two later, so it may not be the way to go. Our lunches will carry you through a long day and provide the energy you need to be at your best late in the afternoon. Many of these lunches can be prepared quickly in the evening and stored in the refrigerator for a grab-and-go nutritious lunch the next day.

DINNER should be a time when you can sit and enjoy a meal without time constraints. Whether you eat at home or go out with friends, it's a time to nourish your soul after a long day. Our dinner recipes will be simple meals, which take around 10 or so minutes to prepare, leaving you plenty of time to enjoy a relaxing evening while still enjoying a good meal. If preparing food for others, remember to make your meal first so you are not tempted to eat off the 21-day menu. If dinner is not usually a relaxing time for you, look into how you can change this dynamic. Be mindful and in the moment, as most things can wait while you nourish yourself. When you are strong and healthy, you can better serve others.

SNACKS are what may have taken you down the wrong path to begin with. The good news is Raw-Vitalize snacks are not only yummy, but they are good for you compared to most other snacks. Quickly made, they will be a blessing in disguise when you feel the need for a quick pick me up. Remember a great piece of fruit makes a wonderful snack as well. Buy seasonal fruits and eat them when fully ripe. Let fruit ripen on the kitchen counter instead of in the refrigerator. A good-quality, juicy, ripe fruit is luxurious and our snacks will keep you satisfied. No guilt indulgence necessary.

DESSERTS are one of the best parts of life and if you like sweets you will really love these recipes. A small amount will fill your desires because they are full of nutrients, which will satiate you faster than non-raw desserts. Who ever thought the words nutrients and desserts could be used in the same sentence? Dessert recipes are made for more than one serving. They will be refrigerated or frozen so when you feel the urge for a sweet, it will be ready with just a little time out of the freezer—or in some cases eaten immediately. We advise you to make one or two of the desserts the first week so you will have them throughout the 21 days to grab when you feel like having a little treat. Our healthy desserts can help you avoid cravings for unhealthy desserts.

From the women who have gone there before you, we present Raw-Vitalize.

2

THE
21-DAY PLAN

WEEK ONE

	BREAKFAST	SNACK	LUNCH	SNACK	DINNER
DAY 1	Chia Pudding	Snack or Smoothie	Sweet Potato Swirls	Snack or Smoothie	Buddha Bowl
DAY 2	Tropical Paradise with Cashew Cream	Snack or Smoothie	Super Amazing Heirloom Tomato Salad	Snack or Smoothie	Zucchini Ribbons
DAY 3	Hardy Harvest	Snack or Smoothie	Zucchini Hummus Wrap	Snack or Smoothie	Stuffed Portobello Mushroom
DAY 4	Apple Sunrise	Snack or Smoothie	Detox Glow Salad	Snack or Smoothie	Cheesy Noodles
DAY 5	Superfruit Bowl with seeds	Snack or Smoothie	Tapas Salad	Snack or Smoothie	Zucchini Ravioli
DAY 6	Quick Granola with Almond Milk	Snack or Smoothie	Creamy Thai Soup	Snack or Smoothie	Tri-colored Sweet Pepper Salad
DAY 7	Breakfast Pudding	Snack or Smoothie	Kale Caesar	Snack or Smoothie	Warm Curried Cream of Carrot Soup

For shopping convenience, take a photo of the weekly shopping list with your phone. Snacks, desserts, and smoothies are not on the weekly shopping list, as we have left this up to you to make the choice of which ones you want for the week. We suggest you snap a photo of the desired snack, dessert, and smoothie recipes and use that as an add-on to your shopping list.

If you purchased all the items on the Pantry Staples list, you will not need everything on the weekly shopping list and can go directly to the produce department. If you have leftover produce from the previous week, you will not need to purchase those items again.

SHOPPING LIST

Nuts and seeds from Pantry Staples

Almonds

Cashews

Chia seeds

Flaxseeds

Gluten-free oats

Hemp heart seed

Nutritional yeast

Pine nuts

Pumpkin seeds

Sunflower seeds

Walnuts

Spices, seasonings, and nonperishables from Pantry Staples

Almond butter

Black olives

Capers

Cardamom powder

Chili flakes, dried

Chili powder

Cider vinegar

Cinnamon powder

Coconut flakes (unsweetened)

Coconut milk

Cumin powder

Dijon mustard

Dried cranberries or raisins

Extra-virgin olive oil

Maple syrup

Medjool dates

Onion powder

Paprika powder

Sundried tomatoes, no oil

Tahini

Tamari

Vanilla, pure extract

Produce Department

Apple, red: 1; green: 1

Arugula: 1 bag or small bunch

Avocados: 3

Bananas: 2

Basil, fresh: 2 bunches

Beet: 1 small

Bell peppers, orange:1; red: 2, yellow: 1

Berries: 16 ounces

Cabbage, purple or white: 1; savoy: 1

Carrots: 8

Celery: 1 stalk

Corn: 1 ear or 1 bag organic frozen

Cucumbers, English: 3; Persian: 1 carton

Garlic: 2 bulbs

Ginger root: 3- or 4-inch piece

Grapefruit: 1

Green onion: 1 bunch

Italian parsley: 1 bunch

Jalapeño: 1

Kale: 1 bunch

Lemons: 6

Lemongrass: 1 stalk

Limes: 2

Mushrooms: 3 medium baby bellas

Papaya: 1

Pineapple: ½ (if only a whole pineapple is available, cut in half and freeze the other half to use in smoothies)

Romaine leaves: 1 bunch

Rosemary: 1 bunch fresh or 1 jar dried

Shallots: 1 bunch

Spinach: 8 ounces

Sweet potatoes: 2 medium

Tomatoes, cherry: 1 small carton; Heirloom: 2; red: 1

Thyme: 1 bunch fresh or 1 jar dried

Zucchinis, green: 4 medium; yellow: 2 small

WEEK TWO

	BREAKFAST	SNACK	LUNCH	SNACK	DINNER
DAY 8	Chia Seed Cranberry Oat Bar	Snack or Smoothie	Amazing Caesar Salad	Snack or Smoothie	Guacamole Veggie Sticks
DAY 9	Detoxifying Green Lemonade Smoothie	Snack or Smoothie	Chop Chop Hooray	Snack or Smoothie	Sweet Corn Chowder
DAY 10	Mango Pudding	Snack or Smoothie	Friends of the Nori Roll	Snack or Smoothie	Vitality Soup
DAY 11	Banana Smoothie Bowl	Snack or Smoothie	Chopped Thai Salad	Snack or Smoothie	Stuffed Cremini Mushrooms
DAY 12	Fruit Smoothie Bowl	Snack or Smoothie	Stuffed Tomato	Snack or Smoothie	Collard Rollups
DAY 13	Mono Fruit	Snack or Smoothie	Street Taco	Snack or Smoothie	Zucchini Ribbons with Italian Arrabbiata Checca
DAY 14	Superfruit Bowl with Seeds	Snack or Smoothie	Avocado Vessel	Snack or Smoothie	Warm Spicy/Mild Chili

Ta-da! Week two will be even more fun than week one. You've got the hang of it now. A straightforward shopping list, leftover ingredients, your preferred desserts, snacks, and smoothies will make things even easier. This week will fly by and you will have a whole new list of favorite recipes to use forever.

SHOPPING LIST

Nuts and seeds from Pantry Staples

Almonds

Cashews

Chia seeds

Flaxseeds

Gluten-free oats

Pecans

Pumpkin seeds

Sunflower seeds

Walnuts

Spices, seasonings, and nonperishables from Pantry Staples

Black olives

Cayenne pepper

Coconut water

Dried cranberries, cherries, or raisins

Dulse

Green tea

Hemp seeds

Italian seasoning

Medjool dates

Pumpkin pie spice or cinnamon powder

Sesame oil

Sundried tomatoes, no oil

Vegan Mayo

Produce Department

Apples, red; 3; green: 3

Avocados: 6

Bananas: 5

Basil: 1 bunch

Bean sprouts: 1 handful

Bell peppers, red: 4; yellow: 2

Berries: 16 ounces

Carrots: 6

Celery: 1 stalk

Chives: 1 bunch

Cilantro: 1 bunch

Collard leaves: 2

Corn: 1 ear or 1 bag organic frozen

Cucumbers, English: 2; Persian: 1

Dark leafy greens: 1 bunch

Dill: 1 bunch fresh or 1 jar dried

Fruit of choice: mono (breakfast)

Garlic: 2 bulbs

Ginger root: 3- or 4-inch piece

Jalapeños: 2

Kale: 1 bunch

Kiwi: 1

Lemons: 5

Lemongrass: 1 stalk

Limes: 4

Mangos: 3

Mint: 1 bunch

Mushrooms, cremini: 8; Portobello: 1 medium

Oranges or grapefruit: 2

Pineapple: 4 ounces

Red onion: 1

Romaine lettuce: 1 bunch

Scallions: 1 bunch

Shallots or sweet onion: 1

Snap peas: ½ cup

Spinach: 1 bunch

Tomatoes, cherry: 1 carton; heirloom: 4 medium

Thyme: 1 bunch fresh or 1 jar dried

Zucchinis: 2

You might not need all the ingredients on the list if you previously purchased Pantry Staples. Take a photo of the shopping list and a photo of any smoothies, snacks, or desserts you might want to add to this week's menu.

WEEK THREE

	BREAKFAST	SNACK	LUNCH	SNACK	DINNER
DAY 15	Chocolate Chia Pudding	Snack or Smoothie	Tri-Color Sweet Pepper Salad	Snack or Smoothie	Pad Thai
DAY 16	Nut Seed and Fruit Bowl	Snack or Smoothie	Jicama Fries with BBQ	Snack or Smoothie	Tomato, Cucumber Sweet Onion Salad
DAY 17	Mono Fruit	Snack or Smoothie	Oh So Good Simple Sandwich	Snack or Smoothie	Curried Coconut Pasta Bowl
DAY 18	Banana Vanilla Smoothie	Snack or Smoothie	Apple, Red Cabbage Beet Salad	Snack or Smoothie	Warm Noodle Soup
DAY 19	Gogi Berries and Oats	Snack or Smoothie	Nut Butter, Banana, Vegetable Wrap	Snack or Smoothie	Veggie Chop Salad
DAY 20	Banana Pudding	Snack or Smoothie	Yellow Squash with Asian Sauce	Snack or Smoothie	Filled Sweet Red Pepper
DAY 21	Banana Smoothie Bowl	Snack or Smoothie	Salad In a Jar	Snack or Smoothie	Kale Shreds with Cashew Ranch

Zip-a-dee-doo-dah! Can you believe you are here at week three already? You are doing great! This is your week to soar. Honestly if we were you right now, we would be patting ourselves on the back.

SHOPPING LIST

Nuts and seeds from Pantry Staples

Almonds

Cashews

Chia Seeds

Flaxseed

Gluten-free oats

Hemp heart seeds

Pumpkin seeds

Sunflower seeds

Walnuts

Spices, seasonings, and nonperishables from Pantry Staples

Cacao powder

Chili flakes or cayenne powder

Chili powder

Coconut water

Curry powder

Goji berries

Herbs de Provence

Medjool dates

Smoked paprika

Sundried tomatoes

Turmeric powder

Produce Department

Apples, Granny Smith: 2; red: 1

Avocados: 2

Bananas: 4

Basil: 1 bunch

Bean sprouts: 1 handful

Beets: 2

Bell peppers, orange: 1; red: 4; yellow: 2

Berries: 16 ounces

Broccoli: 1 stalk

Cabbages, purple: 1; savoy or green, 1; white: ½

Carrots: 5

Celery: 1 stalk

Cilantro: 1 bunch

Collard leaves: 4

Corn: 2 ears, or 1 bag organic frozen

Cucumbers: 2

Daikon radish: 1

Dill: 1 bunch fresh or 1 jar dried

Fruit of your choice: mono (breakfast)

Garlic: 1 bulb

Ginger root: 3- or 4-inch piece

Jícama: 1

Kale: 1 bunch

Lemons: 5

Lettuce, Romaine: 1 bunch

Limes: 3

Mint: 1 bunch

Mushrooms, Shiitake dried: 4

Onion, red: 1; sweet: 1

Oranges: 3

Oregano: 1 bunch fresh or 1 jar dried

Scallions: 1 bunch

Shallots: 1 bulb

Snow peas: 1 handful

Sprouts: 8 ounces

Sweet potato: 1

Tomatoes, cherry: 1 container; heirloom: 2; large tomato: 1

Thyme: 1 bunch fresh or 1 jar dried

Zucchinis: 6

You might not need all the ingredients on the list if you previously purchased Pantry Staples. Take a photo of the shopping list and a photo of any smoothie, snack, or dessert recipes in the book you might want to add to this week's menu.

3

THE RECIPES

BREAKFAST

Chia Pudding

Tropical Paradise with Cashew Cream

Hardy Harvest

Apple Sunrise

SuperFruit Bowl

Quick Granola and Almond Milk

Breakfast Pudding

Chia Seed Cranberry Oat Bar

Green Detox Smoothie

Mango Pudding

Banana Smoothie Bowl

Fruit Smoothie Bowl

Mono Fruit

Chocolate Chia Seed Overnight Pudding

Nut Seed and Fruit Bowl

Banana Vanilla Smoothie, or Mono Fruit

Goji Berries and Oats

Banana Pudding

CHIA PUDDING
BREAKFAST, DAY 1
SERVES 1

NOTE: Prepare the pudding the night before so it will be ready in the morning.

Chia seeds are both delicious and healthy. Just because chia pudding is creamy, with little bursts of jelly-like seeds, there's no reason you should feel guilty about eating this for breakfast. These powerhouse seeds are loaded with antioxidants, protein, calcium, magnesium, and fiber. See photo on page 51.

FOR THE CHIA PUDDING

1 cup almond milk (recipe follows or use store-bought)

3 level tablespoons chia seeds

2 or more teaspoons maple syrup or sweetener of choice (no white sugar)

Berries or fruit of choice

METHOD

Pour milk into a bowl or jar with a lid. Add chia seeds and whisk, stir, or shake to disperse the seeds and keep them from clumping together. Let the mixture rest for 10 minutes and whisk, stir, or shake again to break up any lumps. Whisk in sweetener until well combined. Repeat whisking in another 10 minutes, then store in the refrigerator at least 4 hours, or overnight. In the morning, add berries or other desired fruits and seeds.

be realistic, expect miracles.

FOR THE ALMOND MILK

MAKES 3 CUPS ALMOND MILK (RECIPE FOLLOWS)
SOAK TIME FOR ALMONDS 8+ HOURS OR OVERNIGHT

NOTE: Allow 8 hours or more for almonds to soak before making almond milk. You will have 3 servings of almond milk from this recipe to use throughout this first week. If possible, make the almond milk and chia pudding in the evening so they will be ready for breakfast the next day.

If you haven't made almond milk before, it's very simple. It is healthy and tastes far better than cow's milk. If you don't have time to make your own, you can purchase almond milk at your supermarket. The product you purchase has been processed, so it's not raw and may contain sugar—check the ingredients to be sure the milk you purchase is free of sugar. In our experience, there is a vast difference between homemade and store-bought almond milk. Boxed almond milk doesn't taste anywhere near as rich and creamy as homemade and, of course, the homemade version is much healthier because it hasn't been processed or preserved with additives. Give the homemade version a try and we think you will love the silky smooth results. Milk will last 3 to 4 days in the refrigerator.

INGREDIENTS

1 cup almonds, soaked for 8+ hours or overnight and rinsed

3½ cups filtered water

2 Medjool dates, pits removed

1 splash pure vanilla extract

METHOD

Blend rinsed almonds, filtered water, dates, and vanilla until almond pieces disappear, about 3 minutes. Strain the milk from the almond pulp by pouring the liquid into a nut filter bag (can be purchased at most health food stores or online) or a clean cotton dishtowel that has been placed over a bowl. Hold the top of the bag tightly closed while you squeeze the liquid into the bowl with your other hand. Squeeze firmly at the end to extract all the milk. Store milk in a glass container with a tight-fitting lid. Pulp can be dehydrated to make almond flour or you can freeze the pulp for later to use in cookies and breads.

TRY THIS TIP

A sprinkle or two of cinnamon or cardamom makes a great addition.

TROPICAL PARADISE WITH CASHEW CREAM
BREAKFAST, DAY 2

SERVES 1

NOTE: Cashews should be soaked for 2+ hours. They can be soaked the day before, rinsed well, and kept in a tight-lidded jar in the refrigerator until ready for use. Best used in two days.

This colorful fruit array, with its creamy, rich-tasting sauce, can make your day seem very decadent—and why shouldn't it be that way? Fruit is the nectar of the Gods and we marvel in the nutrients, antioxidants, and vitamins they provide us. If you can take a moment before devouring this dish, just think about all the sun and water that went into the making of the fruit. It's a miracle, right?

FOR THE TROPICAL PARADISE

We are suggesting tropical fruits, as we love this combination. Feel free to use any fruit or berries you like. The Cashew Cream goes well with all fruits, including apples, oranges, berries, or whatever is in season.

INGREDIENTS

Cashew Cream (recipe follows)

½ papaya

½ cup pineapple

1 banana

METHOD

Prepare Cashew Cream. When ready to serve, peel fruit and cut into bite-size pieces. Arrange fruit on a plate or in a bowl. Pour desired amount of Cashew Cream on top. This is a great dish to prepare the night before and store in a glass container as a grab-and-go in the morning.

This will make more than one serving and can be kept in the refrigerator for three days. Cashew Cream is so good you might want to fix this a second day. Use any extra on fruit or in a smoothie. You might catch yourself with a spoon at the refrigerator looking for the leftover cream.

INGREDIENTS

1 cup cashews, soaked for 2+ hours and rinsed

2 Medjool dates + 2 teaspoons maple syrup or just 1½ tablespoons maple syrup

1 tablespoon lemon juice

2/3 cup filtered water

METHOD

Place all ingredients in blender and blend until smooth. Cashew Cream firms up a bit when refrigerated or you can add a couple drops of filtered water and stir to desired texture.

TRY THIS TIP

Any extra fruit can be frozen for smoothies.

HARDY HARVEST
BREAKFAST, DAY 3
SERVES 1

NOTE: Oats need to be left for 1 to 2 hours or overnight in the refrigerator. It is best to soak the oats the night before.

Sometimes the simplest foods turn out to be the best. This is a solid, jam-packed, post-workout breakfast, which is tasty and crowded with vitamins and nutrients. We chose more exotic fruits for a touch of sophistication and juiciness, but all fruits are good for you, so buy what you like or what's in season.

INGREDIENTS

½ cup gluten-free oats, soaked for 1–2 hours, or overnight

1 cup almond milk, ¼ cup reserved for topping (see page 53)

½ teaspoon cinnamon or cardamom

1 teaspoon pure vanilla extract

A pinch sea salt

1–2 teaspoons maple syrup or sweetener of choice (no white sugar)

1 persimmon, papaya, mango, or other fruit of choice

1 tablespoon hemp, sunflower, or pumpkin seeds, or a combination of all three

METHOD

Place oats, 3/4 cup almond milk, cinnamon, vanilla, salt, and sweetener in a food processor and pulse chop until incorporated. Place in a serving bowl and refrigerate overnight. In the morning, add chopped fruit and seeds. Serve with ¼ cup of almond milk.

TRY THIS TIP

If taking on the go in the morning, store the oat mixture in a jar with a tight-fitting lid. Chop fruits and combine seeds and berries in a separate container and assemble when ready to eat.

APPLE SUNRISE
BREAKFAST, DAY 4
SERVES 1

This recipe sounds almost too simple to be so good, but that's the whole idea—simple and healthy. Apples are loaded with a variety of nutrients. They boost your immune system, fight cancer, and are good for your brain. Almond butter contains healthy monounsaturated fats and can keep your blood sugar stable. It's rich with all kinds of good vitamins, and to say the least, it's good for your heart and powers your body. This is just a purely delicious, easy recipe. See photo on page 48.

INGREDIENTS

1 heaping tablespoon raw almond butter

1 apple, roughly chopped into large chunks

1 handful berries of choice, for topping

1 tablespoon flaxseeds, for topping

Fresh berries or dried cherries, cranberries, goji berries, or raisins, for topping

METHOD

Place almond butter and apple chunks into a food processor. Pulse chop until apples are chopped into small, bite-size pieces, but not mashed. Remove mixture from food processor and place into a bowl. Add in berries and sprinkle on flaxseed. Top with fresh berries or dried cherries, cranberries, goji berries, raisins, or a mixture of all.

SUPERFRUIT BOWL
BREAKFAST, DAYS 5 AND 14

SERVES 1

Start your day on a happy note with a variety of fruit to activate your senses and nourish your skin and cells. Vitamin C is one of the stars of this dish. Seeds bring the mineral zinc, which will boost your immunity and ensure good sleep. Seeds are a good source of protein and the fat is the good kind that your body needs. In addition to the health benefits, your taste buds will be delighted.

INGREDIENTS

1 apple

1 orange or grapefruit

1 kiwi

1 generous handful blueberries or other berries

1 tablespoon sunflower seeds

1 tablespoon pumpkin seeds

1 tablespoon flaxseeds

METHOD

Chop apple into bite size pieces. Peel and cut orange or grapefruit into bite-size pieces. Remove any seeds and arrange citrus in a bowl. Cut kiwi in half and scoop out fruit with a teaspoon and add to the bowl. Add berries and sprinkle on the seeds. This is a great dish to prepare the night before and store in a glass container to grab-and-go in the morning.

QUICK GRANOLA AND ALMOND MILK
BREAKFAST, DAY 6
SERVES 1

Brighten up your morning with nutty, crunchy granola and ice-cold almond milk. Double this recipe if you would like to keep some on hand for a snack during the week. Seeds and nuts are a healthy addition to our daily wellbeing. They contain a host of beneficial nutrients, vitamins, minerals, and good fats, which work to strengthen our heart and brain as they help to decrease our waistline.

NOTE: Whenever possible, soak nuts and seeds for 2+ hours before consuming. They digest more easily and plump up nicely, making them more hydrated. After soaking, rinse well before using. If you don't have time to soak ahead, you can still make this recipe.

INGREDIENTS

1 tablespoon roughly chopped almonds

1 tablespoon roughly chopped walnuts

1 teaspoon sunflower seeds

1 teaspoon pumpkin seeds

1 teaspoon flaxseeds

1 teaspoon hemp heart

1 teaspoon raisins or dried cranberries

⅓ cup almond milk (see page 53)

METHOD

Place all ingredients in a bowl and add almond milk. If you are taking this on the go, store nuts and seeds in a jar with a tight-fitting lid and bring almond milk in a separate container. When ready to eat, pour almost milk into the nut/seed container.

TRY THIS TIP
Feel free to use a drizzle of maple syrup on top.

BREAKFAST PUDDING
BREAKFAST, DAY 7

SERVES 1
SOAK CASHEWS 2+ HOURS

Pudding for breakfast is a novel idea. What makes this acceptable is that all the ingredients are good for you. The cashews make the pudding creamy and the chia seeds are little bubbles of pure protein. We used cashews for this pudding because, unlike almonds, you do not have to strain the pulp from the liquid. Best to soak the cashews 2+ hours before using, if possible. Make this recipe in the evening and refrigerate for an on-the-go breakfast.

INGREDIENTS

½ cup cashews, soaked for 2+ hours and rinsed

1 cup + 3 tablespoons filtered water

1 frozen or ripe banana

½ cup berries of choice

2 teaspoons maple syrup or more to taste

1 splash pure vanilla extract

2 tablespoons chia seeds

METHOD

Place everything except the chia seeds into a blender and blend until very smooth. Pour into a jar and whisk in chia seeds. Let rest for 10 minutes, then whisk again to keep the seeds from clumping up. Wait another 10 minutes, whisk, and put the lid on the jar and refrigerate to chill. Eat immediately or store in refrigerator.

CHIA SEED CRANBERRY OAT BAR
BREAKFAST, DAY 8
MAKES 6 BARS

Energy bars make the perfect breakfast or snack and are great to grab on the go as you dash out the door for your busy day. They can give you the needed boost in case of a slump in the middle of the day or keep you going if you miss a meal.

INGREDIENTS

¼ cup cashews

½ cup almonds

2 tablespoons chia seeds

½ cup pumpkin seeds

¼ cup sunflower seeds

1 cup Medjool dates

¾ cup gluten-free oats

1 teaspoon pure vanilla extract

¼ cup dried cranberries, cherries, or raisins

1 pinch sea salt

1 teaspoon pumpkin spice or ⅛ teaspoon cinnamon and ⅛ teaspoon cardamom

METHOD

Place nuts and seeds into a food processor and pulse into small pieces. Add dates and chop again until mixture sticks together when pinched. Add more dates if necessary. Place mixture into a bowl and add oats, vanilla, and cranberries, salt, and pumpkin spice. Combine thoroughly. Line an 8 x 8-inch baking dish with parchment paper and press mixture evenly to sides of dish. Refrigerate overnight. Remove from refrigerator and cut into 6 even bars. Wrap each bar in plastic wrap and store in a zip-lock bag in refrigerator or freezer for up to four weeks.

GREEN DETOX SMOOTHIE
BREAKFAST, DAY 9
SERVES 1

We think you will enjoy this boost of greens. Greens are not just for salads, so we've put together a smoothie packed with essential vitamins and minerals. Easy to make and take with you to work for an energetic day ahead.

INGREDIENTS

1½ cups filtered water, chilled green tea, or coconut water

2 frozen bananas, broken in pieces

2 handfuls spinach

2 kale leaves, stems removed

1 orange, peeled, seeded, and broken into pieces

1 teaspoon hemp seeds

METHOD

Blend all ingredients, adding more water if necessary.

NOTE: If you use non-frozen bananas, add 4 ice cubes to the blender.

MANGO PUDDING
BREAKFAST, DAY 10
SERVES 1

It's clear by now that we are fans of pudding for breakfast because it's quick, flavorful, and easy to transport to work or the gym. Mangos are rich, creamy, and make great ice cream, so if you would like to freeze this pudding for that purpose, go right ahead. Remove it from the freezer 10 minutes before eating. Mangos will give you that extra boost of all things good, as far as vitamins and minerals are concerned. Pudding should be made in the evening, so it will be ready for breakfast the next day.

INGREDIENTS

1 mango, peeled and pitted

¼ cup cashews, soaked for 2+ hours and rinsed if possible

1 tablespoon + 1 teaspoon maple syrup or liquid sweetener of choice
(no white sugar)

Juice from ½ lime

2 tablespoons coconut oil

2 tablespoons filtered water

METHOD

Blend all ingredients until very smooth. You want to keep the mixture as thick as possible. but if you need to thin it, add 1 teaspoon water at a time to make it smooth. Pudding will firm up in the refrigerator. Taste and add more sweetener to taste.

BANANA SMOOTHIE BOWL
BREAKFAST, DAYS 11 AND 21
SERVES 1

Is this a breakfast or a dessert? Either way, it'll make you happy. Freezing ripe bananas was a great discovery. Just peel and break into a couple of pieces and store in a freezer bag—no more wasted bananas. This smoothie bowl is so delicious, you will be thrilled to see spotted bananas on your countertop, just waiting to be frozen. Think of all the potassium you will receive too.

INGREDIENTS

1 frozen banana

1 green apple

1 tablespoon almond butter

½ teaspoon maple syrup (optional)

1 tablespoon almond milk (see page 53) or filtered water

1 small handful sunflower seeds, for topping

1 small handful pumpkin seeds, for topping

2 teaspoons flaxseeds, for topping

1 tablespoon raisins, for topping

1 dash cinnamon and cardamom, for topping

1 drizzle maple syrup, for topping

METHOD

Chop banana into chunks. Put the banana, apple, almond butter, and optional maple syrup into a food processor and pulse until smooth and creamy, adding almond milk or water as needed to make a smooth texture.

Place banana mixture into a bowl and add toppings.

FRUIT SMOOTHIE BOWL
BREAKFAST, DAY 12
SERVES 1

Having a tasty breakfast helps the day look more positive. A beautiful Fruit Smoothie Bowl is packed with goodness. It's important to get your daily fruit consumption, which will ensure you get the nutrients you need to keep you energetic throughout your day.

INGREDIENTS

1 cup pineapple, berries, mango, or any frozen fruit you have in the freezer

½ frozen banana

1 green apple

1 tablespoon almond butter

1 drizzle maple syrup, if desired

1 tablespoon almond milk (see page 53) or filtered water

1 small handful sunflower seeds, for topping

1 small handful pumpkin seeds, for topping

METHOD

Put the pineapple, banana, apple, almond butter, and optional maple syrup into a food processor and pulse chop until smooth, adding almond milk or water as needed to make mixture smooth but thick as possible. Place into a bowl. Place fruit mixture in a bowl and sprinkle with toppings.

MONO FRUIT

BREAKFAST,
DAYS 13, 17, AND 21

You can choose any fruit, which could
include a cup or more of berries,
two or more bananas, or
seasonal stone fruits.

CHOCOLATE CHIA SEED OVERNIGHT PUDDING
BREAKFAST, DAY 15

SERVES 1

Prep this before you go to bed and your dreams will come true in the morning. Yes, we are saying chocolate for breakfast. You will be using cacao powder, which has been called a superfood and delivers high amounts of antioxidants to help combat free radicals. Raw cacao powder has 20 times more antioxidants than blueberries and contains calcium carotene, magnesium, protein, thiamin, riboflavin, and essential fatty acids. No guilt and all good for you. Expect to enjoy a chocolaty, decadent, and nutrition-rich breakfast.

INGREDIENTS

1 ¼ cups almond milk (see page 53)

3 ½ tablespoons chia seeds

2 tablespoons cacao powder

1 tablespoon maple syrup, plus more for optional topping

1 pinch salt

2 teaspoons unsweetened coconut flakes, for topping

Fresh berries, for topping

METHOD

Add all ingredients except berries and coconut flakes to a mason jar and thoroughly mix together. Place the lid on the jar and store overnight in the refrigerator. When ready to eat, add berries, coconut flakes and more maple syrup, if desired, to taste. Let the day begin!

NUT SEED AND FRUIT BOWL
BREAKFAST, DAY 16

SERVES 1
SOAK SEEDS AND NUTS 1+ HOUR, IF POSSIBLE

Simple elements create delightfully wonderful tastes and textures. Take time to chew your meals well and you might just have a new experience of flavors you never noticed before. Your digestion will improve along with your appreciation for the straightforward taste of fresh and natural, uncomplicated food.

INGREDIENTS

¼ cup sunflower seeds

2 tablespoons pumpkin seeds

1 tablespoon hemp seeds

6 cashews or 2 tablespoons cashew pieces, chopped

6 almonds, roughly chopped

2 Medjool dates, cut into pieces

1 teaspoon raisins

1 apple, diced into small pieces

1 tablespoon almond butter

1 dash cinnamon

Juice of 1 orange

½ cup fresh berries of choice

METHOD

Place sunflower, pumpkin, and hemp seeds in a bowl, cover with filtered water, and soak 1 hour or more. In a second bowl, place cashews, almonds, dates, and raisins and cover with filtered water. Soak for 1+ hour. Rinse all soaked ingredients and set aside. Place apple and almond butter in a bowl, mix well to combine, and sprinkle in cinnamon. Combine apple mixture with seeds and nuts. Transfer to a large serving bowl and add freshly squeezed orange juice. Place fresh berries on top and add more cinnamon, if desired.

BANANA VANILLA SMOOTHIE
BREAKFAST, DAY 18
SERVES 1

Start today with one of your smoothies (pages 182–89). If you froze them ahead of time, remove one from the freezer and let it sit overnight in your refrigerator. It should be ready to drink in the morning. If you did not make a smoothie ahead, try this very simple one.

INGREDIENTS

1½ cups filtered water or coconut water

1 frozen or fresh banana

1 small handful cashews

3 Medjool dates or 1 tablespoon maple syrup

1 teaspoon pure vanilla extract

1 orange, peeled and quartered

4 ice cubes

METHOD

Put all ingredients, except the ice, in a blender and blend until smooth. Add ice and blend again.

Alternatively, eat a mono fruit, which means choose one fruit and eat as much of it as you want. Choose from any fruits in season including watermelon, papaya, apples, or a large bowl of berries and eat at as much as you like.

TRY THIS TIP

Toss in a couple handfuls of dark, leafy greens into your smoothie, such as spinach, romaine, or kale. Sprinkle seeds of choice on top of the blended drink for garnish.

GOJI BERRIES AND OATS
BREAKFAST, DAY 19
SERVES 1

Goji berries make a great snack. These shriveled berries contain vitamins C, B2, A, iron, antioxidants, and selenium. They are good for eye health and are known to boost the immune system and brain activity. Goji berries protect the heart and improve life expectancy. They might seem new to us, but the Tibetans have used goji berries for traditional medicine for over 1,700 years.

INGREDIENTS

⅓ cup gluten-free rolled oats

2 tablespoons goji berries

2 tablespoons roughly chopped walnuts

1 tablespoon hemp seeds

1 dash cinnamon

Almond milk (see page 53), if desired

Maple syrup or sweetener of choice (no white sugar), if desired, to taste

METHOD

Place oats and goji berries in a bowl, cover with filtered water about 2 inches above the oats/berries, and soak for 1 hour or until softened. Oats and berries can be soaked in the evening, rinsed, and placed in a tight-fitting jar with a lid. They will be ready to use in the morning.

TO ASSEMBLE

Place the goji berries on top of the oats along with the walnuts and hemp seeds. Sprinkle on cinnamon and add almond milk. If desired, add maple syrup to taste.

TRY THIS TIP

Place a tablespoon of goji berries in a 16-ounce jar of filtered water and sip the water throughout the day. Eat the berries when the water is finished.

BANANA PUDDING
BREAKFAST, DAY 20
SERVES 1

You can rule the world if you start your day with fulfilling nutrients. Energy and brain-power are very important when you have to make decisions throughout your day. This breakfast will take you where you need to go and keep you satisfied all morning.

INGREDIENTS

1 ripe banana

1 tablespoon almond butter

1 small handful pumpkin seeds

1 small handful sunflower seeds

A little squeeze of lemon

1 dash cinnamon, for topping

METHOD

Mash banana in a bowl, add almond butter, and mix in. Add pumpkin and sunflower seeds and mix in. Squeeze on lemon, top with cinnamon, and chill or eat immediately.

LUNCH

Sweet Potato Swirls

Super Amazing Heirloom Tomato Salad

Zucchini Hummus Wrap

Detox Glow Salad

Tapas Salad

Creamy Thai Soup

Kale Caesar

Amazing Caesar Salad

Chop Chop Hooray

Friends of the Nori Roll

Chopped Thai Salad

Stuffed Tomato

Street Taco

Avocado Vessel

Tri-Colored Sweet Pepper Salad

Jícama Un-Fries With Barbecue Dipping Sauce

Oh So Good Simple Sandwich

Apple, Purple Cabbage, and Beet Salad

Nut Butter, Banana, and Veggie Collard Wrap

Noodle Combo with Asian Sauce

Salad in a Jar

SWEET POTATO SWIRLS
LUNCH, DAY 1
SERVES 1

The color alone can make your day brighter. Sweet potatoes are bursting with vitamin C, which helps accelerate collagen and aids in maintaining your skin's youthful elasticity. You can count on sweet potatoes, too, for vitamin D, iron, magnesium, and potassium. The natural sugars in sweet potatoes are slowly released into the bloodstream, helping to ensure a balanced and regular source of energy to carry you through your busy day. If you've invested in a spiral slicer (spiralizer) by now, you've done yourself a big favor. It's a great way to cut back on harmful pasta carbs and have a delicious meal ready in minutes. A spiralizer is an amazing kitchen tool that can turn zucchini, carrots, sweet potatoes, kohlrabi, and apples into noodles in just minutes. There are other methods for making noodles if you don't have a spiralizer. You can make strips with a potato peeler, then lay the strips on top of each other and cut the strips into thinner noodles, if preferred. There is also a julienne peeler, which looks similar to a potato peeler but has thin spikes across the blade to make thin strips. A mandoline or bread slicer will slice zucchini into strips, which can be placed into a stack and cut with a sharp knife into thinner noodle strips. Anyway you cut it, this dish will be memorable. See photo on page 81.

FOR THE SALAD

1 medium-size sweet potato (alternatively, yams or butternut squash can be used)

½ cup basil, ribbon cut

¼ cup corn or approximately ½ ear of corn kernels

METHOD

Peel sweet potatoes and spiralize if possible. It's easier to spiralize when sweet potatoes are cut evenly in half with a flat end on both sides. Alternatively, use a potato peeler and make fettuccini-type noodles. Cut spiralized noodles to desired length. Place in a mixing bowl and add basil and corn.

FOR THE DRESSING

1½ tablespoons tamari

1 tablespoon cider vinegar

2 teaspoons maple syrup, or to taste

1 teaspoon peeled and grated ginger

1½ tablespoons raw almond butter

2 tablespoons + 1 teaspoon extra-virgin olive oil

½ large garlic clove, finely chopped if using blender or crushed if whisking

1 pinch dried chili flakes, to taste

METHOD

In a blender or small mixing bowl, blend or whisk all ingredients until smooth.

TO ASSEMBLE

Pour dressing on top of the sweet potato noodles and toss until noodles are coated. Place in a serving bowl or on a plate to enjoy.

TRY THIS TIP

Add hijiki or other soaked seaweed to the noodles for an umami flavor.

you are in charge of your own fork!

◊ ◇ ◊

SUPER AMAZING HEIRLOOM TOMATO SALAD
LUNCH, DAY 2

SERVES 1

Heirloom tomatoes can be found in a variety of colors. They have a short season, but if you can bag yourself a few, you will truly love them. During off-season, find a perfectly ripe tomato that speaks to you. It's really okay if you pick them up and see how they feel. A slight give is much riper than a hard one and so much more flavorful. Ripe fruits and vegetables will yield the best flavor and vitamins. Many farmers' market tomatoes have that great smell whereas some supermarket tomatoes have no smell at all. We know you are busy, but choosing the best produce is one of the little pleasures in life to cultivate.

FOR THE SALAD

1 large heirloom tomato (when in season or the best-looking tomato you can find)

1 small cucumber

1 small avocado

¼ cup chopped or torn dulse (sea vegetable)

4–5 basil leaves, ribbon cut

METHOD

Dice heirloom tomato and cucumber into bite-size pieces. Place in a mixing bowl. Cut avocado in half and discard pit. Cube avocado in its skin and scoop cut pieces into the bowl. Add dulse and basil leaves.

FOR THE DRESSING

1 tablespoon extra-virgin olive oil

Juice of 1 lime

Tiny pinch cayenne pepper (optional)

1 garlic clove, crushed

1 pinch sea salt and black pepper, to taste

Whisk together all the ingredients. Taste and adjust salt and seasonings as necessary.

Combine dressing with the salad and lightly toss. Place on a beautiful plate or bowl. If you are making this salad the night before to take to work, do not add dressing until ready to eat. Place salad into a mason jar and store in refrigerator. Show yourself some extra love and bring a pretty bowl along to pour your salad into at work.

ZUCCHINI HUMMUS WRAP
LUNCH, DAY 3
SERVES 1

Here is our friend the limitless zucchini showing off its diversity again. Easy to digest, raw zucchini hummus will give you a new take on the traditional dish made with garbanzo beans. Garbanzo beans can make a raw hummus if they are sprouted, but using zucchini is lighter and faster. We are serving it up here as a wrap, but its also delicious as a dip with crudités or to top a salad. See photo on page 22.

FOR THE HUMMUS

1 large zucchini or 2 small ones

½ cup tahini

1 tablespoon extra-virgin olive oil

1 garlic clove, cut in half or crushed

1 tablespoon lemon juice

1–2 pinches sea salt, to taste

1 teaspoon cumin

Sprinkle of paprika, for topping

METHOD

Peel zucchini, cut the ends off, and slice into chunks. Place all ingredients in a food processor except the paprika. Pulse ingredients until creamy and thick. Taste and adjust seasonings. Place in a glass storage container and sprinkle on paprika. If you have any leftover hummus, store in refrigerator for 2 to 3 days.

TRY THIS TIP

Add other fresh herbs, sundried tomatoes, red bell peppers, and a drizzle of olive oil.

6 strips julienne-cut carrot

6 strips julienne-cut red bell pepper

6 strips julienne-cut cucumber

4 strips mango (optional)

Choice of sprouts (optional)

FOR THE WRAP

2 savoy or white cabbage leaves

METHOD

Pare down the hard core of the cabbage leaves as flat as possible. Use a scissor if necessary to shape down the size of the leaves. A collard or romaine leaf will also make a lovely wrap.

TO ASSEMBLE

Place desired amount of hummus on the leaf and lay vegetables on top. Fold leaf over to eat. If taking to work, fold leaf over and wrap in plastic wrap or wrap both separately and fill when ready to eat.

DETOX GLOW SALAD
LUNCH, DAY 4
SERVES 1

All the ingredients in this salad will help to purify you body and make your skin glow. We can't hydrate enough and our body needs water and hydrating foods. Many skin eruptions are from an acidic body that lacks hydration. We added seeds for protein to make a well-balanced lunch that will keep you light and energetic in the middle of the day.

FOR THE SALAD

1 cup coarsely chopped spinach, kale, or arugula, or a combination of all

1 small carrot

½ small beet

½ green apple

1 small cucumber, peeled and diced

1 small avocado or ½ medium avocado, diced (ripe but not too soft)

1 green onion, white and green part chopped

1 tablespoon pumpkin seeds

1 tablespoon sunflower seeds

1 tablespoons chopped walnuts

¼ cup chopped Italian parsley leaves

METHOD

Wash and spin or towel dry dark greens. Peel carrot and beet. Here is where you have three choices for preparing the veggies. Choose whichever is easiest and quickest for you. You can shred the carrot and beet along with the green apple in a food processor if you have that attachment blade. Alternatively, you can pulse the carrot, beet, and apple separately into bite-size pieces. Your third choice is to chop ingredients finely with a sharp knife. Place prepared ingredients in a mixing bowl. Place cucumber, green onion and avocado dices in the bowl. Toss in pumpkin seeds, sunflower seeds, and walnuts. Add chopped parsley leaves.

RECIPE CONTINUES

2 tablespoons lemon juice

2 tablespoons extra-virgin olive oil

1 tablespoon cider vinegar

4 teaspoons maple syrup or liquid sweetener of choice (no white sugar)

1 large garlic clove, crushed

1 tablespoon finely chopped fresh dill, or 1 teaspoon dried dill

A few grinds or pinch sea salt and pepper, to taste

METHOD

Place all dressing ingredients in a jar with a tight lid and shake vigorously. Pour desired amount onto the chopped vegetable and seed mixture and gently toss. Reserve 1 tablespoon to toss into the greens if you are eating right away. See tip below if you are taking it to go.

TO ASSEMBLE

Arrange the dark leafy greens in a serving bowl and toss with reserved 1 tablespoon dressing. Mound the dressed chopped vegetables and seed mixture on top. The salad can be made in the evening and stored in a mason jar with a tight-fitting lid—it makes a great grab-and-go meal to take to work.

TRY THIS TIP

If placing salad into a jar, place dressed, chopped mixture in the jar first followed by the dark leafy greens. When ready to eat, pour salad into a bowl. The greens will stay crisp and the dressing from the vegetables will be enough to moisten the greens.

TAPAS SALAD
LUNCH, DAY 5
SERVES 1

If you enjoy some of the refined flavors from south of the border, then you will love this light version of classic ingredients. All the tastes playfully come together in the dressing and the crunch lies in the salad. If the saying "We eat with our eyes" is true, then there is a feast awaiting you. Walnuts have the distinction of looking like our brain, hence it is said that walnuts support good brain health. Along with other healthful benefits, walnuts are an excellent source of anti-inflammatory omega-3 essential fatty acids.

FOR THE VESSEL

2 whole red or white cabbage or romaine leaves

METHOD

Pare down the hard core of the cabbage leaves as flat as possible. Use scissors if necessary to shape down the size of the leaves.

FOR THE FILLING

1 cup walnuts

¼ red bell pepper, coarsely chopped or broken into pieces

⅛ teaspoon cumin

1 dash chili powder

1–2 dashes onion powder

1 pinch sea salt and pepper

METHOD

Pulse filling ingredients in a food processor to break down into smaller pieces. A little chunk is fine.

RECIPE CONTINUES

1 cup seeded and diced tomato

½ cup diced cucumber

¼ cup chopped cilantro

½ celery rib, chopped

½ small avocado, diced

1 jalapeño, chopped (size depending on your spice preference)

FOR THE DRESSING

2 tablespoons extra-virgin olive oil

⅛ teaspoon cumin

1 garlic clove, crushed

2 tablespoons lemon juice

Sea salt and pepper, to taste

METHOD

In a small bowl, whisk together all the dressing ingredients. In a large bowl, toss dressing with salad ingredients. Taste and adjust seasonings if necessary.

TO ASSEMBLE

Place filling in cabbage cups and spoon salad on top. Add extra slices of jalapeño if desired.

CREAMY THAI SOUP
LUNCH, DAY 6
SERVES 1

You won't be disappointed with this creamy soup. In fact, this might become one of your favorite go-to meals when looking for an abundance of Thai flavor in one single spoonful. The extra crunch brings it all together, supplying additional nutrition. If you like a little extra spice, a pinch of chili pepper will do the trick.

1 cup coconut milk

¼ cup almond milk (see page 53)

2-inch shallot

1 celery rib

1 green onion

1 tablespoon lemon or lime juice

1 tablespoon extra-virgin olive oil

1 garlic clove

½ apple

⅛ teaspoon curry powder

⅛ teaspoon cumin

1 teaspoon peeled and chopped ginger

1 tablespoon chopped basil

1 tablespoon cilantro

1 tablespoon tamari

1 handful unsweetened coconut flakes

1–2 pinches sea salt, or to taste

Fresh ground black pepper, to taste

Chopped basil, cilantro, green onion, and a dash of paprika, for topping (any or all)

METHOD

Add all the ingredients except for the optional toppings to a blender. Blend until smooth. Taste and add more salt if necessary. This soup likes to be a tad salty.

TRY THIS TIP

Try this as a noodle soup! Spiralize zucchini noodles and cut them into 1-inch pieces to add to the soup.

KALE CAESAR
LUNCH, DAY 7
SERVES 1

How did kale become so popular? How did kale become the farm-to-table superfood? The word "kale" is even on one of Beyoncé's T-shirts. Since 2007, kale production increased 60 percent. Oddly enough, kale has been around for 2000 years, but up until recently, Pizza Hut was the largest buyer—they used it to decorate the edges of their salad bars. Today, there is even a National Kale Day. Bon Appétit ran an article in 2009 on kale chips made by a famous New York Chef. And aside from Dr. Oz saying kale was healthy and Gwyneth Paltrow making baked kale chips on *Ellen*, *Time* magazine called it the top food trend of 2012. Research now proves that kale became popular through guerilla marketing. Let's all be happy kale because it's currently considered one of the healthiest greens we can consume. Hale kale!!

FOR THE SALAD

3 cups de-stemmed and large, ribbon-cut kale

1 teaspoon lemon juice

1 pinch sea salt

½ teaspoon extra-virgin olive oil

¼–½ cup corn (to be added when assembling salad)

METHOD

Place kale in a bowl and massage the pieces with lemon juice, salt, and olive oil to slightly soften.

RECIPE CONTINUES

1 garlic clove, crushed

2 teaspoons crushed or well-chopped capers

2 tablespoons lemon juice

1 teaspoon tamari

¼ teaspoon Dijon mustard

2–3 tablespoons extra-virgin olive oil

Sea salt and pepper, to taste

2 tablespoons Parmesan Nut Cheese (see page 101)

METHOD

Whisk together all dressing ingredients until well incorporated or place all ingredients in a jar with a tight-fitting lid and shake vigorously.

TO ASSEMBLE

Toss massaged kale and corn with desired amount of dressing. Add more Parmesan Nut Cheese to your liking. This salad holds up well overnight when refrigerated—it makes a great grab-and-go lunch. Seal in an airtight container or jar with a tight-fitting lid.

AMAZING CAESAR SALAD
LUNCH, DAY 8
SERVES 1

Simple cold, crisp lettuce is complemented with a dressing loaded with flavor. Just enough of the right ingredients to remember how good a perfect salad can be. There are many recipes the whole family would love, but this one in particular is always a big hit. Toss the dressing in just before ready to eat to keep the lettuce crisp.

FOR THE SALAD

Romaine lettuce

Use any amount of romaine lettuce leaves. Romaine hearts have a firm texture and hold up well to a weighty dressing. Save the softer outer leaves for lettuce wraps or juicing.

METHOD

To get crisp, cold lettuce, wash and wrap lettuce leaves in paper towels or a clean cotton kitchen towel and place in the refrigerator to crisp and dry for at least 1 hour. You can even freeze your salad plate for added chill.

FOR THE DRESSING

2 garlic cloves, crushed

½ cup extra-virgin olive oil

⅛ teaspoon tamari

1–2 teaspoon mashed or crushed capers (use a garlic press to crush)

Juice of ½ large lemon or lime

⅛ teaspoon Dijon mustard or a generous 1–2 pinches mustard powder

Sea salt, to taste

Freshly ground black pepper, to taste

¼ cup or more Parmesan Nut Cheese (recipe follows)

RECIPE CONTINUES

In a small mixing bowl, whisk all the dressing ingredients together, except the Parmesan Nut Cheese. When all ingredients are incorporated, whisk in the Parmesan Nut Cheese. Dressing should be on the thick side. This recipe will make more than you need, but the remainder can be saved for another salad.

TO ASSEMBLE

Remove chilled lettuce from the refrigerator and slice lettuce into bite-size pieces. Place lettuce in a large salad bowl and add dressing a little at a time. Give the salad a bath with the dressing but don't drown it. Toss lightly. Add more dressing if necessary to your desired taste. Sprinkle on more Parmesan N Cheese.

PARMESAN NUT CHEESE

Cashew Parmesan Cheese will become a staple in your refrigerator. Use it to perk up salads and pastas.

INGREDIENTS

1 cup cashews (do not soak)

1 garlic clove, halved

Sea salt, to taste (should be lightly on the salty side)

METHOD

Place all ingredients in food processor and pulse chop into fine pieces until it looks the consistency of Parmesan cheese. Scrape down sides with a spatula when nuts stick around the bottom. Do not over pulse or you will have cashew butter. Place in glass container with a tight-fitting lid and store in refrigerator 2-3 months.

CHOP CHOP HOORAY
LUNCH, DAY 9
SERVES 1

Combine a couple of our favorite ingredients and you'll realize that a very tasty dish does not have to be complicated. In this recipe, great textures mingle with a lemony dressing to make a perfectly light, satisfying meal.

FOR THE CHOP CHOP

1 small zucchini, small diced

1 dash sea salt

1 splash lemon juice

Drizzle of extra-virgin olive oil

¼ cup red bell pepper, small diced

¼ cup corn

½ avocado, small diced + 3 extra-thin crescent moon slices for topping

1 tablespoon basil, ribbon chopped, for topping

METHOD

Place diced zucchini into a bowl and toss in a little salt, lemon juice, and olive oil to help release extra water. Let rest 10 minutes. Drain any liquid from the bowl and add diced avocado. Place red pepper and corn in a separate mixing bowl.

FOR THE DRESSING

½ tablespoon lemon juice

1 teaspoon extra-virgin olive oil

1 drizzle maple syrup or sweetener of choice (no white sugar)

1 tablespoon basil, ribbon chopped

½ tablespoon minced scallion

Sea salt and pepper, to taste

METHOD

Whisk all dressing ingredients together and taste for any adjustments.

TO ASSEMBLE

Place drained avocado mixture into the bowl with the red pepper and corn. Add dressing to the mixture and lightly toss in. Set a 3-inch ring mold on a plate and press chopped ingredients into mold. Lift mold off and garnish with 3 thin slices of avocado, ribbon-cut basil, and a drizzle of olive oil. In place of a ring mold, mound ingredients in the center of a bowl and garnish as directed.

FRIENDS OF THE NORI ROLL
LUNCH, DAY 10

MAKES 2 NORI ROLLS
SERVES 1

Making a pâté for a Nori roll is quite easy. It's a good place to let your imaginary creative friend loose in the kitchen to help you. Once you learn the basics, you can set yourself free with different spices and herbs. Taste is important, as is texture, and Nori rolls have it all—crunchy, creamy, and juicy all in one bite. You might want to have some fresh pâté around at all times for a quick roll up or to use in a salad or Buddha bowl.

FOR THE PÂTÉ

½ cup peeled and roughly chopped carrots

½ cup pecans

¼ cup pumpkins seeds

1 tablespoon roughly chopped shallot or sweet onion

½ cup roughly chopped red sweet bell pepper

¼ cup dulse

1 tablespoon cider vinegar

2 teaspoons lemon juice

½ tablespoon tamari

1 pinch sea salt, or to taste

2 tablespoons chopped fresh dill or 1 tablespoon dried

METHOD

Pulse-chop all pâté ingredients in a food processor until well incorporated into a smooth paste, scraping down sides of the food processor when needed. Taste and adjust seasonings if necessary.

RECIPE CONTINUES

⅛ teaspoon wasabi, or more if you like it spicy

1 tablespoon tamari

Mix together wasabi and tamari for the dipping sauce. Set aside.

2 raw nori sheets

¼ cucumber, peeled, seeded, and sliced into thin matchsticks

½ avocado, thinly sliced

¼ red bell pepper, cut into thinly sliced matchsticks

If you have a sushi bamboo mat use it. Alternatively, spread a sheet of plastic wrap on your chopping board vertically. Lay the nori sheet on the prepared surface with the shiny side down and the lines on the nori running horizontal. Spread half the pâté evenly over ⅔ of a nori sheet, leaving an inch on the end closest to you. Spread the pâté all the way out to the side edges. Arrange cucumber, avocado, and red bell pepper on top of the pâté at the end closest to you, bringing the vegetables all the way to the side edges. Take a hold of the plastic wrap and bring up the edge of the nori to start rolling. When you have completed the first roll and covered the veggies, give a light squeeze on the wrap to secure the roll. Lift the edge of the plastic wrap and continue to use the plastic wrap to finish rolling, applying a little pressure for a tight roll. Roll until ½-inch of nori is left exposed, then lightly wet your finger and run it across the exposed nori. Continue rolling and lightly squeeze to seal and shape roll using the plastic wrap. Remove the plastic wrap and place the roll on the chopping board seam side down. Cut in half with a sharp or serrated knife. Repeat directions to make a second. Roll. Serve with the dip.

CHOPPED THAI SALAD
LUNCH, DAY 11

SERVES 1

Life, like food, needs to be balanced. Thai dishes reflect Thai culture's attention to detail and variety. Texture, color, and good flavor are what make a dish show its finest side. As with all our recipes, we place an emphasis on medicinal benefits as well as taste. The Chopped Thai Salad is about simplicity and creating harmony with fresh natural ingredients.

FOR THE DRESSING

2 tablespoons + 2 teaspoons extra-virgin olive oil

1 large garlic clove, peeled

⅛ cup cashews

1½ tablespoons tamari

1 tablespoon filtered water

1 tablespoon cider vinegar

1 tablespoon maple syrup or sweetener of choice (no white sugar)

½ tablespoon sesame oil

½ tablespoon peeled chopped ginger or a peeled 1-inch piece

1-inch piece lemongrass (as an alternative, use a squeeze of lemon)

Squeeze of lime juice

METHOD

Puree all the dressing ingredients in a food processor or blender until smooth, adding water a little at a time, if necessary, for a thick creamy texture. Taste and adjust ingredients to fit your preferences. Transfer to a dressing jar with a tight-fitting lid. This recipe makes two to three servings of dressing, so you can refrigerate the rest for use in other salads.

RECIPE CONTINUES

2 cups baby romaine, thinly sliced (for a larger salad, add another cup romaine)

1 small carrot, shredded into strips with a peeler

¼ red bell peppers, cut into matchstick-size pieces or chopped

¼ yellow bell peppers, cut into matchstick-size pieces or chopped

¼ cup chopped cilantro

1 small scallion, both white and green parts chopped

¼ cup + a little more bean sprouts (optional, as they are not always easy to find)

3–4 tablespoons cashew pieces (not soaked)

TO ASSEMBLE

Place romaine lettuce, carrot strips, bell peppers, cilantro, and scallion into a bowl. Add the desired amount of dressing on top and toss until well combined. Add sprouts and cashews and lightly toss in.

TRY THIS TIP

Do not add dressing until ready to serve. Store extra dressing for another use.

you know more than you give yourself credit for.

STUFFED TOMATO
LUNCH, DAY 12
SERVES 1

Get your camera ready, as beauty is in the Stuffed Tomato. Fresh, fragrant, and bursting with color, this stuffed tomato is overflowing with health. Simple and satisfying is what we get with this dish. The filling is so delicious you might want to use it to top a green salad.

FOR THE TOMATO

Find an heirloom or any large, beautiful tomato. Cut a small slice from the top and, with a paring knife, cut carefully around the inside of the tomato. Use a teaspoon to remove the seeds and spine, leaving a hollow for you to fill.

FOR THE FILLING

½ cup almonds, soaked 2+ hours

½ cup sunflower seeds, soaked 2+ hours

1 garlic clove, crushed and chopped

1 tablespoon fresh dill, or ½ tablespoon dried dill

1 celery rib, chopped

2 scallions, white and green parts chopped or ¼ cup chopped sweet onion

1 teaspoon lemon juice

⅛ teaspoon Dijon mustard

1 tablespoon chopped dulse or other sea vegetable

2 tablespoons vegan mayo, or more if desired (recipe follows)

Sea salt and pepper, to taste

METHOD

Rinse nuts and add to a food processor. Pulse into small chunks. Scrape nuts into a mixing bowl.

Combine the rest of the filling ingredients with the nuts. Turn in a bit of mayo. Taste and add more salt or pepper if necessary.

Fill the hollow of the tomato with the stuffing and add a dollop of mayo on top. Snap your photo and eat.

VEGAN MAYONNAISE

This recipe will make more than you need for this dish, but you will be using it throughout the 21 days.

INGREDIENTS

⅛ cup filtered water, plus another ⅛ cup if needed for blending

1 cup cashews, soaked for a creamier consistency, 2+ hours and rinsed

1 garlic clove

¼ cup chopped cauliflower

2 tablespoons lemon juice

1 teaspoon maple syrup

1 tablespoon cider vinegar

1–2 dashes onion powder

Sea salt, to taste

1 teaspoon Dijon mustard

¼ cup extra-virgin olive oil

METHOD

Blend all ingredients but the oil. Once mixture is smooth and thick, pinch between your fingers to make sure there is no grit left. Continue blending and add oil slowly through the opened lid of the blender. Taste and adjust any seasonings if necessary. Store in refrigerator in a tight-lidded jar. Mayo will be used in other recipes.

STREET TACO
LUNCH, DAY 13
SERVES 1

Let's be clear: These are not intended to be authentic street tacos. This recipe doesn't include corn tortillas or animal products, and in a real street taco, you won't find lettuce or tomato inside. Our street taco is a bit different, but we think it's really delicious. For the taco filling, we use rich-tasting sundried tomatoes combined with walnuts, cumin, and chili. We replace the tortilla with crisp romaine lettuce, add some complementary veggies, and top it all with Creamy Cashew Sour Cream. This healthy version of a street taco will have you dreaming of the beauty and fun to be had south of the border.

FOR THE TACO NUT FILLING

¼ cup tightly packed sundried tomatoes, soaked 2+ hours until soft

½ cup walnuts

1 good pinch garlic powder

1 good pinch cumin

1 good pinch chili powder

1 gentle pinch cayenne, to taste

Sea salt and pepper, to taste

METHOD

Remove tomatoes from soaking and reserve water. Place all ingredients into a food processor and pulse until well-incorporated but still maintaining texture.

FOR THE CREAMY CASHEW SOUR CREAM

½ cup cashews, soaked 2+ hours and rinsed

1½ teaspoons lemon juice or ⅛ teaspoon cider vinegar

1 pinch sea salt, or to taste

3 tablespoons filtered water, plus more as needed

METHOD

Place all ingredients into blender. Begin by adding 3 tablespoons of water to make a thick, smooth, and creamy sour cream; add more water if needed a little at a time. Start your blender on low and increase speed once the mixture is blended. If you put it on high immediately, the ingredients will fly up on the sides. You will have to scrape sides down occasionally to be sure mixture is smooth without small nut pieces.

FOR THE VEGGIES

2 romaine lettuce leaves, for the taco wrap

½ avocado, sliced

1 small tomato, chopped

¼ cup chopped cilantro

1 scallion, finely chopped

A few small leaves of arugula

TO ASSEMBLE

Spread spoonfuls of Taco Nut Filling on lettuce leaves. Place avocado slices on top along with the tomato, cilantro, scallion, Creamy Cashew Sour Cream, and arugula.

TRY THIS TIP

If you are taking this dish to work, assemble when you are ready to eat. Carry each item in a separate jar or container. Keep cold romaine lettuce leaves wrapped in paper towels to stay crisp and refrigerate until ready to use.

AVOCADO VESSEL
LUNCH, DAY 14
SERVES 1

Avocado is the only fruit that contains monounsaturated fatty acids—the good fats. It's loaded with potassium and fiber, and is known to lower cholesterol. With its super health benefits, avocado can be called fruit of the Gods. With more potassium than a banana, it contains vitamins B1, B2, B3, B5, B6, B9, C, E, K, mineral salts, copper, iron, magnesium, and phosphorus. Relax, new findings claim avocado consumption will not make you fat—that idea is so yesterday, or should we say so 1980s. Avocado is heart healthy, and, as we mentioned, is full of the good kind of fat, so eating some daily is a good idea as it actually helps curb hunger. "An avocado a day keeps the doctor away" should be the new slogan. For a little fun, if you would like to grow your own avocado tree, here's what to do: Wash the avacado seed, push 3 toothpicks into the seed and suspend the seed, wide end down, in a glass filled with water. Place the glass in a warm place with sunlight, if possible. Keep water about an inch above the seed and refill water when necessary. The seed will sprout roots and leaves in three to six weeks. If it doesn't sprout in that amount of time, discard and try another seed. When the roots reach six inches, cut back to three inches and continue growing until more green leaves show. Plant in good humus soil, leaving half the pit showing. Water, but don't saturate.

FOR THE VESSEL

1 large ripe avocado, cut in half and pitted

1 tomato, seeded and finely diced

2 radishes, finely chopped

¼ large cucumber or English cucumber, finely chopped

1 scallion, finely chopped

METHOD

Prepare avocado and set it aside. Place remaining chopped ingredients into a mixing bowl.

2 tablespoons lemon juice

1 tablespoon extra-virgin olive oil

1 pinch sea salt and pepper

1 tablespoon fresh dill or ½ teaspoon dried dill

METHOD

Whisk all of the dressing ingredients together until well combined.

TO ASSEMBLE

Toss dressing into vegetables. Fill each cavity of avocado with salad.

TRI-COLORED SWEET PEPPER SALAD
LUNCH, DAY 15

SERVES 1

The simplest foods can be loaded with flavor. This ultra-vibrant salad has a satisfying crunch. When we eat a rainbow of colors, we are getting a full variety of nutrients. Complement this salad with a delightfully light dressing and lunch or dinner become a harmonious treat. This dish is great by itself or tossed on top of a handful or two of arugula.

FOR THE SALAD

½ each red, yellow and orange bell pepper, thinly sliced

1 small zucchini, thinly sliced

2 tablespoons finely chopped sweet onion

METHOD

Remove seeds and white parts from the inside of the peppers. Slice the peppers and zucchini into matchstick-size pieces. Place into a bowl and add chopped onion.

FOR THE DRESSING

3 tablespoons extra-virgin olive oil

¼ teaspoon oregano

¼ teaspoon thyme

1 teaspoon fresh basil, ribbon cut

Juice of ½ lemon

Sea salt and pepper, to taste

METHOD

Place all dressing ingredients into a bowl and whisk together to emulsify.

TO ASSEMBLE

To the bowl of dressing, add the sliced peppers, zucchini, and onions. Toss. Place in a serving bowl and eat.

JÍCAMA UN-FRIES WITH BARBECUE DIPPING SAUCE

LUNCH, DAY 16

SERVES 1

Accentuate the flavor of an almost-flavorless tuber and a great surprise is in store. Crunch is such a great word, and crunchy food is very satisfying and enjoyable. When you were a kid, did you ever love to order French fries and a Coke? Now we can have both flavor and health. We don't recommend washing down your jícama fries with a Coke, but you could toss a little crushed fresh ginger in some bubbly water with a squeeze of lemon and a dash of maple syrup and it just might remind you of your carefree days.

If you're not familiar with the tuber jícama and its bark-like skin, it might seem like an intimidating root at first. To describe the taste, we would say it's crunchy, sweet, and juicy, and is usually eaten raw with lemon or lime and possibly some chili powder. You can find it at many supermarkets especially Latin American, Mexican, or Asian markets. Jícama needs to be peeled before eating. A potato peeler doesn't seem to work as well as a good sharp knife. Cut off both ends and following the curve of the jícama, place your knife under the skin, and peel it, cutting where necessary to remove any hard outer fibers. A potato peeler can work at this point to remove hard fibers. Just run a peeler over the white flesh. Jícama makes a great veggie served with vegetable dips and guacamole, and chopped in salads. If you can't find jícama, you can substitute with kohlrabi, turnip, or rutabaga, which are also root vegetables—but there is nothing quite like jícama, so it's worth the effort to locate one.

FOR THE FRIES

1 medium jícama, peeled

1 scallion, white and green part finely chopped

1 tablespoon extra-virgin olive oil, and, if needed, a little more to coat the fries

⅛ teaspoon paprika powder

1 tablespoon chili powder

⅛ teaspoon onion powder

Sea salt, to taste

RECIPE CONTINUES

Cut peeled jícama into even vertical slices, then cut those into French-fry–size pieces. Place all ingredients in a bowl and toss very well to coat thoroughly. Cover bowl and place in refrigerator for about an hour to marinate.

FOR THE BARBECUE SAUCE

¾ cup sundried tomatoes, soaked 1–2 hours until soft

2 tablespoons cider vinegar

1 small garlic clove

1 scallion, white and green part, rough chopped

2 Medjool dates, rough chopped

½ tablespoon maple syrup

⅛ teaspoon Dijon mustard

½ teaspoon tamari

1 teaspoon lemon juice

1–2 dashes onion powder

1–2 dashes smoked paprika powder

Cayenne pepper, to taste

Sea salt and pepper, to taste

½ cup sundried tomato soaking water, plus more if needed

METHOD

Take tomatoes out of the soaking water, reserving water. Place tomatoes and remaining ingredients into a blender and blend until very smooth, adding more tomato soaking water as necessary for proper texture. Barbecue sauce should be thick, smooth, sweet, and hot. More cayenne pepper may be needed to suit individual taste.

TO ASSEMBLE

Remove jícama fries from the refrigerator, arrange in a bowl or on a plate, and place barbecue sauce in a small bowl for dipping.

OH SO GOOD SIMPLE SANDWICH
LUNCH, DAY 17
SERVES 1

It's hard to imagine this recipe being as satisfying as it is. You might want to eat this three days in a row it's so good. It could not get any easier. The crunch and the creaminess along with the sharp sweetness of the onion makes this the perfect oh so good sandwich. See photo on page 39.

INGREDIENTS

2 leaves savoy, Asian, or standard green cabbage

Soy-free vegan mayonnaise, or some left over from recipe on page 111

6 thin slices avocado

4 cucumber rounds, peeled and thinly sliced

2 thin slices sweet or red onion

2 thin slices tomato

1 pinch sea salt

TO ASSEMBLE

Cut down the hard core of the cabbage leaves as flat as possible with a paring knife. Spread mayo on both leaves, lay 3 slices of avocado on each leaf, and add cucumber, onion, and tomato slices. Add a pinch of salt and you have a ready-to-eat, open-face sandwich. And yes, it's perfectly okay if you want to make one more!

APPLE, PURPLE CABBAGE, AND BEET SALAD
LUNCH, DAY 18
SERVES 1

This combination of vegetables and fruit will have you energetic in no time. All the flavors and nutrients come alive when combined in one bowl. This salad reminds you to chew your food and take time to enjoy your lunch. A few minutes for "you" can make the rest of the day feel more alive. You will be creative and energetic with immune-boosting beets loaded with vitamin C, apples with potassium, vitamins K and B6, riboflavin, and copper. Add in cancer-fighting cruciferous cabbage, which is also known to decrease the risk of diabetes, obesity, and heart disease, promotes a healthy complexion, and you have a lunch worth living for.

FOR THE SALAD

¾ cup thinly sliced and lightly packed purple cabbage

1 small beet, peeled sliced into thin rounds, then cut into thin strips

1 Granny Smith apple, cored and sliced into thin rounds, then cut into thin strips

1 tablespoon finely diced red onion

¼ cup roughly chopped walnuts

6 mint leaves, chopped

Sea salt, to taste

METHOD

Prepare ingredients, place in a mixing bowl, and salt lightly.

FOR THE DRESSING

2 tablespoons extra-virgin olive oil

2 tablespoons cider vinegar

2 teaspoons maple syrup or sweetener of choice (no white sugar)

Sea salt and black pepper, to taste

Whisk together and taste. Add more sweetener or salt and pepper if needed.

TO ASSEMBLE

Place desired amount of dressing on salad and toss. Mound salad into a large bowl. Salad may be chilled for 15 minutes or eaten immediately.

NUT BUTTER, BANANA, AND VEGGIE COLLARD WRAP

LUNCH DAY 19

MAKE 3–4 WRAPS

SERVES 1

Collard leaves have traveled far from their native Mediterranean background. Historical accounts of collards are mentioned in Ancient Greece and Ancient Rome, after which time they headed to France and England. Somehow they ended up being a staple on the plates of Southerners in America. Collards provide vitamins B6, C, A, and K, and are rich in a host of minerals. They may help prevent cancer and carry carcinogens out of the body. Eat your greens and stay healthy!

FOR THE WRAP

4 collard leaves

4 teaspoons raw almond butter, divided

½ large avocado

½ ripe banana

½ cup sprouts of choice, or chopped romaine

½ cup shredded carrots

½ cup shredded beets

½ red bell pepper, cut into thin strips

2 scallions, green and white parts cut into strips

4 teaspoons sunflower seeds

Wash leaves and pat dry with a clean cotton kitchen towel or paper towel. Use a knife to carefully remove the thick stem from the leaves. Rub leaves with a little lemon juice and salt to slightly soften if necessary, or run under warm water. Some collard leaves can be quite large, so use whole or remove the center stem and use the sides for the wrap.

Lay leaves flat on a chopping board shiny side down. Divide and spread almond butter on the leaves. Mash avocado and banana together and spread on the leaves. Divide sprouts, carrots, beets, peppers, and scallions on top of avocado-banana mixture. Sprinkle on some sunflower seeds.

FOR THE DIPPING SAUCE

¼ cup almond butter

1 tablespoon maple syrup

½ teaspoon lemon juice

1–2 splashes tamari

Warm filtered water, as needed for desired consistency

METHOD

Whisk all ingredients together in a bowl or a blender.

TO ASSEMBLE

As you place the wrap ingredients on the leaf, spread the filling out to the ends of the leaf so when the leaf is finished being rolled, the open sides show some filling. When all ingredients have been added, take one side of the leaf and start to roll tightly. Secure with a toothpick to hold together. Serve with the dipping sauce.

TRY THIS TIP

Feel free to add any leftover veggies you might have on hand. For transporting, wrap each roll in paper towels and place in a container with a lid.

NOODLE COMBO WITH ASIAN SAUCE
LUNCH, DAY 20
SERVES 1

A combination of noodles gives this recipe added texture and taste. Combine yellow and green zucchinis, sweet potato, and daikon radish, or choose one or two of your favorites. The creamy sauce will enhance any veggies you choose for the noodles.

FOR THE NOODLE SALAD

2 cups (approximately) spiralized (or potato-peeled) combination of your choice:
daikon radish, sweet potato, and zucchini

¼ cup shredded red cabbage

¼ cup thin strips red or yellow bell pepper

1 pinch sea salt

METHOD

Turn veggies into noodles using a spiralizer or potato peeler. Shred cabbage with a sharp knife or box grater. Cut peppers into thin strips. Add a pinch of salt and toss together.

FOR THE ASIAN SAUCE

1 teaspoon maple syrup or sweetener of choice (no white sugar)

1 tablespoon cider vinegar

1 teaspoon sesame oil or tahini

1 teaspoon extra-virgin olive oil

2 teaspoons tamari

2 teaspoons lime juice

½–1 teaspoon peeled and chopped ginger

1 small garlic clove, chopped

1 tablespoon cilantro

RECIPE CONTINUES

METHOD

Place all ingredients in a blender and blend until smooth. Alternatively, chop ginger, garlic, and cilantro as fine as possible. Place all ingredients in a jar and vigorously shake to combine. Taste and adjust if necessary.

TO ASSEMBLE

When ready to eat, toss in desired amount of sauce and mix. If not eating immediately, keep sauce in a jar until ready to serve the salad.

TRY THIS TIP

Ask your grocer to cut a daikon into a small piece so you don't have to purchase a whole one, as they can be quite large.

happiness is an activity.

◊

SALAD IN A JAR
LUNCH, DAY 21
SERVES 1

There is a feeling of health and uplift with this combination of colors and textures. Bright green just makes one feel healthier. Add in orange and yellow and it evokes summer in a jar. The fragrant aroma of freshness peaks when the jar is opened and tossed into a bowl.

The idea of this salad is to make it ahead and take it with you to work or on the go. The salad is prepared so you can shake the jar when ready to eat, turn it upside down, and pour it into a salad bowl. By placing the dressing on the bottom of the jar, the more delicate vegetables and leafy greens won't get soggy. Prepare in the evening and grab-and-go in the morning.

Here's our secret to a good Salad in a Jar:

1. Dressing goes in the jar first.
2. Hard chunky vegetables next.
3. Then nuts and raisins or dried cranberries.
4. The greens go in last.

If you don't have time to make a salad every day, make two salads at once and they will last for 2 days refrigerated in a jar with a tight-fitting lid. You can make them the same or switch them up and have a couple different dressing options.

FOR THE DRESSING

1 garlic clove, crushed

Juice of ½ lemon

1 teaspoon tamari

1–2 teaspoons crushed capers

½ teaspoon herbs de Provence

Sea salt and pepper, to taste

3 tablespoons extra-virgin olive oil

RECIPE CONTINUES

Place all ingredients in a small bowl, except olive oil. Slowly add olive oil, a couple drops at a time while whisking to emulsify the dressing. Once you have the emulsifying started—this will be obvious as the dressing will look creamy—you can pour the rest of the oil in a little more quickly. Taste and adjust seasonings if needed.

FOR THE SALAD

⅛ cup corn, about ½ ear

⅛ cup chopped carrot

⅛ cup diced red or yellow bell pepper

⅛ cup peeled, seed, and diced cucumber

⅛ cup finely chopped or shredded purple cabbage

⅛ cup spiralized zucchini

Shredded dark leafy greens of choice, to fill the rest of the jar

TO ASSEMBLE

In a 16-ounce mason jar, place desired amount of dressing in the bottom of the jar. Fill the jar in the order the salad ingredients are listed. Put on the lid and store in refrigerator until ready to eat or take with you on the go.

DINNER

Buddha Bowl

Zucchini Ribbons

Overstuffed Portobello Mushrooms

Cheezy Noodles

Zucchini Ravioli with Sundried Tomato Pesto

Tri-Colored Sweet Pepper Salad

Warm Curried Cream of Carrot Soup

Guacamole with Veggie Sticks

Sweet Corn Chowder

Vitality Soup

Stuffed Cremini Mushrooms

Collard Rollups

Zucchini Ribbons with Italian Arrabbiata Checca

Warm Spicy/Mild Chili

Pad Thai

Tomato, Cucumber, and Sweet Onion Salad

Curried Coconut Pasta Bowl

Warm Noodle Soup

Veggie Chop Salad

Filled Sweet Red Bell Pepper

Kale Shreds with Cashew Ranch

BUDDHA BOWL
DINNER, DAY 1
SERVES 1

A Buddha Bowl is a balanced bowl of nutritional foods. It is easy to toss together, always looks beautiful, and can be made up of any vegetables you have in your refrigerator. The idea is to balance a variety of vegetables, seeds, and fats. They work well for breakfast with fruits and seeds. Use whatever you have on hand. The bowl should be nutritious, balanced, and beautiful to look at. Here is one of our favorite simple versions.

FOR THE KALE BASE

3–4 kale leaves, de-stemmed

1–2 drizzles of extra-virgin olive oil

Squeeze of lemon juice

1 pinch sea salt

METHOD

Break kale leaves into bite-size pieces or ribbon cuts, and add a couple drizzles of olive oil, a squeeze of lemon juice, and a sprinkle of salt. Massage kale with your hands to soften.

½ large carrot, peeled and chopped into small cubes

¼ medium-size sweet potato, peeled and spiralized or sliced into ribbons with a wide peeler

½ cup (or more if desired) red or white cabbage, finely shredded

½ medium-size avocado, thinly sliced

¼ red bell pepper, cut into matchstick pieces

1 teaspoon hemp hearts or pumpkin seeds, for topping

FOR THE DRESSING

2 teaspoons extra-virgin olive oil

1 tablespoon cider vinegar

1 tablespoon tamari

1 small garlic clove, crushed

1 tablespoon nutritional yeast

1 tablespoon almond butter or 1 small handful cashews

Filtered water, as needed for desired texture

METHOD

Place all dressing ingredients in a jar with a tight-fitting lid and shake vigorously until combined. Add more water if necessary, depending on desired texture.

TO ASSEMBLE

Arrange kale in the bottom of a wide-mouth bowl and pile each of the above vegetable ingredients in little mounds. Pour amount of dressing to your liking.

ZUCCHINI RIBBONS
DINNER, DAY 2

Zucchini has high water content and is rich in fiber and low in calories, making it a great food for weight reduction. Zucchini has an array of nutrients, including potassium, folate, vitamin A, copper, and phosphorus. It also has a high content of omega-3 fatty acids, niacin, zinc, B vitamins, and calcium. Zucchini lends itself to many interpretations in foods around the world. This recipe has pizzazz, which is surprising with only six ingredients. We think this will be one of your favorite quick go-to meals.

INGREDIENTS

1 large zucchini, sliced into ribbons using a wide-edge peeler

¼ cup sliced raw black olives or regular black olives

¼ cup pine nuts

Drizzle extra-virgin olive oil

1 pinch sea salt and black pepper

METHOD

Place zucchini, olives, and pine nuts into a mixing bowl and drizzled with extra-virgin olive oil, sea salt, and pepper to taste. Toss well and place in a large serving bowl.

OVERSTUFFED PORTOBELLO MUSHROOMS
DINNER, DAY 3
SERVES 1

The texture of portobello mushrooms lends itself to many raw dishes. Once marinated, the taste goes from good to great. Fill it with the Basil Pesto and you have a gourmet delight. This pesto recipe is very tasty on zucchini noodles as well.

FOR THE MUSHROOMS

3 baby portobello mushrooms

2 tablespoons extra-virgin olive oil, plus more for serving

2 tablespoons tamari

1 small handful arugula, for serving

1 tablespoon of lemon juice plus a lemon wedge for serving

1 sliced cherry tomato, for topping

METHOD

Remove stems and gently wipe mushrooms clean with a damp paper towel to remove any dirt. Place the mushroom caps and stems in a bowl. Spoon olive oil and tamari over the mushrooms, making sure the hollow of the mushroom gets some marinade. If necessary, add a little more olive oil or tamari. Marinate for half an hour or more, turning once to cover the mushroom caps.

RECIPE CONTINUES

¼ cup pine nuts and walnuts combined—or all pine nuts or all walnuts, if preferred

1 cup tightly packed basil leaves

2 small garlic cloves, roughly chopped

1–2 pinches nutritional yeast (optional)

Sea salt and pepper, to taste

1 tablespoon extra-virgin olive oil

METHOD

Place nuts in food processor and pulse 2 to 3 times until broken down. Add basil, garlic, optional nutritional yeast, salt, and pepper. Pulse 3 to 4 times. Scrape down sides and add olive oil through the feed tube and pulse a couple more times. Add ½ teaspoon filtered water if necessary. Taste and adjust salt and pepper.

TO ASSEMBLE

Place arugula in a mixing bowl and drizzle a little olive oil on top. Add a grind of salt and a squeeze of lemon juice and blend with the arugula. Choose a complementary plate and arrange arugula on it. Pile each hollow of the mushroom with pesto and place on the arugula bed. Top each mushroom with a slice of cherry tomato and spoon on a little of the mushroom marinade. Add a little squeeze of lemon from the wedge to each mushroom.

CHEEZY NOODLES
DINNER, DAY 4
SERVES 1

NOTE: Soak cashews for 2+ hours. Cashews are easier to blend and digest if soaked, but if you haven't soaked them, you can still make the recipe.

Yes, it's zucchini again, but this time it's yellow (if possible) and smothered with a delectable cheezy sauce. We know giving up cheese is difficult for many people, but cheese is known to clog the body, and if not organic, it carries hormones and steroids from the animal injections, which doesn't sound so great now, right? Many people are allergic to cheese and don't know it. This recipe will save you all the troubles cheese can cause your body. The creamy cheesy sauce marries beautifully with the noodles. There's life after cheese!

FOR THE NOODLES

1 large or 2 smaller yellow zucchinis

METHOD

Spiralize noodles to make 2 cups, or use a potato peeler to make fettuccini-type noodles.

TRY THIS TIP

Zucchini releases water and it's best to salt and let drain 15+ minutes before using. Do not add the cheese sauce if the noodles are not going to be eaten immediately because the water, which releases from the noodles, will dilute the sauce. The noodles can be made the evening before and kept refrigerated. Alternatively, they can be made during the day, lightly salted and kept covered on the countertop until ready for dinner. Drain off any extra water.

RECIPE CONTINUES

1 cup cashews, soaked for 2+ hours and rinsed

⅔ cup filtered water

2 tablespoons finely minced fresh rosemary, or 2–3 teaspoons dried
(fresh is recommended)

2 tablespoons extra-virgin olive oil

Sea salt and pepper, to taste

1½ tablespoons lemon juice

3 teaspoons tamari

3 tablespoons nutritional yeast

METHOD

Place all ingredients into a blender and blend into a thick cream. Add more water if necessary, but keep it thick and pourable. Taste and adjust seasonings if necessary. For a saltier taste, add another splash of tamari. If too thick, add a teaspoon or two of water. If too thin, add a few more cashews.

TO ASSEMBLE

Place noodles in a bowl and spoon on desired amount of cheezy sauce. Eat as is or warm slightly in a pan on the stove. Do not overheat—you want to keep it raw. Sauce may thicken if overheated. Any leftover sauce can be frozen. Place Cheezy Noodles into a serving bowl and eat with more fresh ground pepper.

ZUCCHINI RAVIOLI WITH SUNDRIED TOMATO PESTO

DINNER, DAY 5

SERVES 1

NOTE: Sundried tomatoes need to be soaked. See the directions in the Sundried Tomato Pesto section that follows.

If you've ever had a garden, you'll know why you might miss a zucchini or two when harvesting. For those not familiar with the elusive zucchini, the reason they are missed is they hide under gigantic leaves. You think you've found all the zucchinis and two days later, you come back to harvest again and—low and behold—there are giant zucchini you never saw before. The largest zucchini on record was 69.5 inches long and weighed 65 pounds. The power of the zucchini has an international pedigree. You can find zucchini almost anywhere in the world. They are so popular, they even have their own special day: National Zucchini Day is August 8th. This is the day to celebrate and sneak some of those extra giant zucchini onto your neighbor's porch. Usually 7 to 8 raviolis are sufficient for a meal.

FOR THE RAVIOLI

1 zucchini, peeled and ends cut off—try to find a fat zucchini for the ravioli round

1 pinch sea salt

2 tablespoons lemon juice

Drizzle extra-virgin olive oil

4 basil leaves, ribbon cut, for topping

METHOD

Cut zucchini in rounds, about ⅛- to ¼-inches thin. Use the largest rounds of the zucchini for the ravioli. If you have a mandoline, this would be the best way to cut them for even, thin slices. Place rounds in a dish and sprinkle with salt, lemon juice, and olive oil. Let marinate for half an hour or more, turning occasionally.

RECIPE CONTINUES

½ cup sundried tomatoes

1 teaspoon lemon juice

1 garlic clove

1–2 Medjool dates

Filtered water as needed

METHOD

Soak the sundried tomatoes in warm water until soft, approximately 1+ hours. They can be soaked the night before, in the morning, or during the day, if you are making this recipe for dinner. Once the sundried tomatoes are fully soaked, rinse them. Pulse all ingredients in a food processor until mixture forms a coarse paste. Add a teaspoon of water if necessary for a little smoother texture. Scrape contents into a small bowl.

FOR THE SAUCE

1 tomato, coarsely chopped

1 garlic clove

¼ small red bell pepper, broken into pieces

¼ cup diced cucumber

1 small pinch sea salt and pepper

½ teaspoon Italian spices

1 teaspoon tamari or 3 black olives

METHOD

Without washing the food processor from the pesto, add all the ingredients and pulse chop until combined. Taste and adjust seasonings if necessary. Pour through a strainer and press lightly to let extra water drain out.

TO ASSEMBLE

Wipe moisture off zucchini slices and arrange slices on a serving plate. Spoon pesto mixture on top of the zucchini rounds and cover with another zucchini round, lightly pressing down. Spoon the tomato sauce on top of raviolis. Top with chopped ribbon cut basil.

TRI-COLORED
SWEET PEPPER SALAD

DINNER, DAY 6

See recipe on page 117, but in addition to
the zucchini, peppers, and sweet onions,
add to this salad ½ a diced cucumber
and a seeded and diced
tomato.

WARM CURRIED CREAM OF CARROT SOUP
DINNER, DAY 7

SERVES 1

Carrots are known for aiding in good eye health, but that's not all. Carrots contain beta-carotene, fiber, and vitamins A, K, and B1. Additional health benefits include folate, potassium, iron, copper, and manganese. All this goodness in one vegetable makes it worth turning it into a soup. Its brilliant color can cheer you on a sunny or cold day.

INGREDIENTS

1½ cups filtered water (or carrot juice, for a richer soup)

1 cup roughly chopped carrots

¼ cup cashews

½ small avocado

1 teaspoon maple syrup or sweetener of choice (no white sugar)

½-inch piece ginger, peeled

½ teaspoon curry powder

Squeeze of lemon or 1-inch piece lemongrass, chopped

1 handful unsweetened coconut flakes

1 teaspoon tamari

Sea salt and pepper, to taste

Extra-virgin olive oil, for topping

Chopped cilantro, for topping

METHOD

Blend water and carrots until smooth. Add remaining ingredients and blend until smooth and creamy. Soup may be warmed slightly on the stove, or if you have a Vitamix blender, use the high setting. Be mindful not to overheat in order to keep it raw. Soup is also delicious at room temperature. Place soup in a bowl, drizzle a little olive oil on top, and a sprinkle of chopped cilantro and ground pepper. This soup also makes a great grab-and-go lunch.

GUACAMOLE WITH VEGGIE STICKS
DINNER, DAY 8
SERVES 1

Leave well enough alone might just apply to guacamole. It's a classic dish that's earned its status because it works so well. Why mess around getting too creative? There have been some dishonorable variations that chefs have tried, but why not just call it something else and leave guacamole out of it? It's not always easy to find ripe avocados, so you have to plan ahead. If you buy them hard, here's what to do to speed up the ripening process. Put one or two avocados in a brown paper bag and add an apple or banana. Seal the bag and in two to three days, the fruit will release gasses, which will ripen the avocados. When you remove the ripe avocados from the bag, it's a good idea to put another one or two hard ones in so they will be ready in time for your next recipe. In this recipe, you will enjoy the creamy texture, which helps discourage cravings. It's served with crisp cold vegetable crudités for a simple sit-on-the-couch-and-watch-TV kind of night.

1 avocado, halved, pitted, and scooped from shell

2 tablespoons finely diced red or sweet onion

Juice of 1 lime

2 tablespoons finely diced tomato seeded

1 tablespoon chopped cilantro

Jalapeño, minced—size depending on heat preference (optional)

1–2 pinches sea salt, to taste

METHOD

Lightly mash avocado with a fork or chop with a wire whisk until smooth. Add onion, lime juice, tomato, cilantro, jalapeño, and salt and gently turn into mashed avocado until well combined. Taste for more salt or lime juice.

FOR THE VEGETABLES

Carrots

Red bell pepper

Cucumber

Snap peas

Celery

METHOD

Cut into large, matchstick-sized dipping pieces.

TO ASSEMBLE

Scoop a mound of the guacamole in the center of a plate and place vegetables around the outside.

TRY THIS TIP

Sorry, no Margarita included, but how about some lime in some bubbly water with a drizzle of maple syrup? You can even blend it for a second with ice for a refreshing drink. Add a mint leaf or two if blending.

SWEET CORN CHOWDER
DINNER, DAY 9
SERVES 1

It's a hearty soup for dinner. Corn and creamy cashews make a very satisfying comfort meal and this soup still leaves a little room for a dessert afterwards. If you use a Vitamix blender you can slightly heat soup in the blender. Alternatively, soup may be warmed lightly on stovetop. We recommend organic corn, which can frequently be found fresh or frozen at supermarkets or health food stores

FOR THE BASE

1 cup corn kernels, reserving 1 tablespoon for topping (see below)

¼ cup cashews

1 garlic clove

1 teaspoon extra-virgin olive oil

¾ cup filtered water or more if needed

¼ avocado

1–2 dashes onion powder

1–2 dashes thyme

1–2 good pinches sea salt

Fresh ground pepper, to taste

1 tablespoon corn kernels, set aside from chowder base, for topping

¼ avocado, diced, for topping

2 tablespoons chopped cilantro, for topping

METHOD

Blend all ingredients, except for toppings. Remember to reserve 1 tablespoon of corn. Taste and adjust seasonings. If the chowder needs thickening, add a few more cashews.

TO ASSEMBLE

Place chowder in a bowl and top with remaining corn, avocado, cilantro, and a grind of black pepper.

VITALITY SOUP
DINNER, DAY 10
SERVES 1

It's good to know that when eating raw food, you are retaining all the nutrients from what-ever you consume. This soup is named properly, as it contains an abundance of vitamins and nutrients to give you vitality. Vitality Soup will surprise you with an extraordinary taste, especially with the addition of a little cayenne pepper. Your body will joyously soak up everything this soup has to offer. If you prefer, soup can be warmed slightly on the stovetop, or use a blender if it has a warming feature. See photo on page 40.

INGREDIENTS

1½ cups coconut water—purchase one without sugar or other additives.

5-inch piece English cucumber

2 celery ribs

1 apple, seeded and roughly chopped

Juice of 1 lime

1 scallion, green and white parts chopped

1 large handful dark leafy greens of choice: spinach, collard, or de-stemmed kale—
or a combination of all three

1 carrot, peeled and roughly chopped

1 small handful dulse

½ avocado

½ red bell pepper

1 small handful fresh assorted herbs of choice: cilantro, mint, parsley, basil

Sea salt and pepper, to taste

1 pinch cayenne pepper (optional)

Place all ingredients into a blender and blend until smooth. Once blended, taste to adjust herbs and seasonings. This is a thick soup. If you like it thinner, add a little more coconut water. Serve in a large bowl, with topings (below), if desired.

FOR THE TOPPING (OPTIONAL)

1 tablespoon seeded and diced tomatoes

¼ avocado, diced

2 tablespoons diced red bell pepper

1 scallion, chopped

1 tablespoon dulse flakes

1 tablespoon chopped fresh cilantro, basil, or mint

○ ○ ○

you cannot love life until you live the life you love.

STUFFED CREMINI MUSHROOMS
DINNER, DAY 11
SERVES 1

NOTE: Sunflower seeds and sundried tomatoes need to be soaked. See the directions in the Stuffing section that follows.

A cremini mushroom is a moderately mature white button mushroom, though not as mature as a portobello, and are sometimes sold as baby bella. They are more flavorful than the white button variety. When purchasing, the underskin should cover the gills. If the mushroom is open to expose the gills, then it is not as fresh. Cremini mushrooms contain vitamins B12 and B6, riboflavin, and niacin along with potassium and beneficial minerals.

8 cremini mushrooms

2 tablespoons tamari

1–2 teaspoons extra-virgin olive oil

1 scallion, finely chopped, for topping

2 teaspoon finely chopped basil, for topping

METHOD

Wipe mushrooms with a damp paper towel and remove stems. Cut off brown ends and finely chop stems. In a small bowl, mix together tamari and olive oil. Marinate mushroom caps and stems in tamari-oil mixture.

FOR THE STUFFING

¾ cup sunflower seeds, soaked 2–3 hours

½ cup sundried tomatoes, soaked until soft, at least 2–4 hours

1 tablespoon lemon juice

1 teaspoon Italian seasonings

1 garlic clove, crushed

Sea salt and pepper, to taste

2–3 tablespoons filtered water, as needed to make a smooth texture

METHOD

Place all stuffing ingredients in a food processor and pulse chop, scraping down sides.

TO ASSEMBLE

Scrape mixture into bowl, add mushroom stems, and lightly mix in. Taste for salt and pepper and add more if needed. Remove mushroom caps from marinade and fill with stuffing. Garnish with scallions and basil. Plate and spoon mushroom marinade over the top.

COLLARD ROLLUPS
DINNER, DAY 12

SERVES 1
MAKES 2 ROLLUPS

Think of this dish as party finger food, a little rollup with a creamy inside. The sturdy collard leaf makes this a great wrap as it holds up very well when all your ingredients are neatly rolled inside.

FOR THE ROLLUPS

2 large collard leaves

½ avocado

1–2 teaspoons Vegan Mayonnaise (see page 111, or use store-bought)

2 tablespoons finely chopped sweet or red onion

6–8 medium-size cucumber matchstick slices

6–8 medium-size red bell pepper matchstick slices

4 medium-size mango slices

Handful of your choice of sprouts or thinly sliced romaine lettuce

Sea salt, to taste

METHOD

Using a paring knife, cut down the hard stems of the collard leaves as flat as possible. Optionally, if you would like softer leaves, soak the collard leaves in very warm water for 15 minutes.

Mash avocado, mayonnaise, and onion together. Place collard leaves shiny side down with the stem closest to you. Divide and spread avocado mixture onto the two leaves, 2 inches from the bottom, spreading to the ends. Evenly divide veggies and place on the avocado mixture. Distribute sprouts, chopped lettuce, and sea salt on top.

TO ASSEMBLE

Start to roll up from the end closest to you. Roll and lightly pull back each time to secure filling. Roll to the end and use a toothpick to hold together.

ZUCCHINI RIBBONS
WITH ITALIAN ARRABBIATA CHECCA
DINNER, DAY 13

SERVES 1

Arrabbiata means angry in Italian. The name of the sauce refers to the spiciness of the chiles. The Italians know about good food, so I hope not to insult them, since our sauce is not cooked, and our pasta is not penne. However, in keeping with tradition, our arrabbiata sauce must taste angry, so spice to your liking and maybe a pinch more.

FOR THE NOODLES

1 large or 2 small zucchini, ribbon-cut with a wide-edge potato peeler

FOR THE ARRABBIATA CHECCA SAUCE

1 cup cherry tomatoes

1 large garlic clove, crushed

1½ tablespoons extra-virgin olive oil or to taste

1 teaspoon capers

¼ cup black olives, roughly chopped

4 large basil leaves, ribbon cut

Sea salt and pepper, to taste

Chili flakes or a pinch of cayenne pepper—as much as you can take

METHOD

Cut tomatoes in half and place in a bowl. Add garlic, olive oil, capers, olives, basil, salt, and pepper. Add chili flakes or a pinch of cayenne pepper to taste. Mix gently together and let sit 10 minutes before topping.

TO ASSEMBLE

Spoon sauce onto zucchini ribbons and gently toss. Use some of the leftover Parmesan Nut Cheese (see page 101) to sprinkle on top.

WARM SPICY/MILD CHILI
DINNER, DAY 14
SERVES 1

NOTE: Sundried tomatoes need to be soaked. See the directions below.

There are many interpretations of this classic dish. If you've ever made your own chili from scratch, you will be familiar with the seasonings and spices. Chili can be very comforting on a cool day. Warming this recipe is the way to go, but it's also delicious at room temperature. Spices are very healthy, so spice it up as much as you like.

INGREDIENTS

½ cup portobello mushrooms

1 small carrot, cut into chunks

½ celery rib, cut into chunks

¼ cup red bell pepper, cut into chunks

¼ cup walnuts

½ cup tomatoes, roughly chopped

½ cup sundried tomatoes, soaked in warm water for 1+ hours or until softened
(can be soaked when you leave for work or overnight)

2 tablespoons chopped sweet onion—taste for strength and add less if necessary

1 garlic clove

½ teaspoon cider vinegar

1 teaspoon tamari

1 teaspoon chili powder, or to taste

½ teaspoon cumin

1 small piece jalapeño, to taste (optional)

Sea salt and pepper, to taste

Filtered water as needed

¼ avocado, diced, for topping

RECIPE CONTINUES

Wipe mushrooms clean, then break into pieces. Place into the bowl of a food processor and pulse until broken down into small pieces. Remove from processor and place into a mixing bowl. To the food processor, add carrots, celery, and red bell pepper, and pulse into small pieces. Add to the mixing bowl. To the food processor, add walnuts, tomatoes, sundried tomatoes, onion, garlic, cider vinegar, tamari, chili, cumin, jalapeño, salt and pepper, and water as needed to arrive at desired chili texture. Pulse ingredients until well combined but chunky. Taste for seasonings and adjust as necessary. Add to the mixing bowl and combine all ingredients.

TO ASSEMBLE

Place desired amount of chili base into a serving bowl and add avocado. Refrigerate for up to 4 days. Chili can be slightly warmed on a stovetop, but be sure not to overheat and cook the ingredients. Store in an airtight container.

TRY THIS TIP

A couple tablespoons of leftover Barbecue Sauce (see page 120)
can be added if desired.

*treat yourself with love
and life just flows.*

PAD THAI
DINNER, DAY 15
SERVES 1

Travel the world for exotic tastes and local color, or, if travel is not on your radar, create a little trip in your kitchen with these Asian noodles. It's exciting to know that just the right combination of ingredients can elevate a meal from good to great. We think you will agree this dressing does just that.

FOR THE NOODLES

1 cup shredded carrots

1 cup shredded zucchini

½ cup thinly sliced red cabbage

¼ cup thin matchstick-cut red bell pepper

½ cup bean sprouts (optional)

½ cup chopped cilantro

10 mint leaves, chopped

1 scallion, white and green part chopped

Juice of ½ lime

3 tablespoons chopped cashews, for topping

METHOD

Prepare all noodle ingredients and place in a bowl. Squeeze lime juice in and toss.

RECIPE CONTINUES

1 small thumb-size knob ginger

1 garlic clove

1 tablespoon tamari

1 tablespoon cider vinegar

1 tablespoon almond butter or ¼ cup cashews

2 tablespoons extra-virgin olive oil

1 tablespoon lime juice

1 drizzle maple syrup or sweetener of choice (no white sugar)

Chili flakes or cayenne, to taste (optional)

Sea salt and pepper, to taste

METHOD

Place all ingredients in a blender or food processor and blend until creamy and smooth. Add orange juice or water if needed for texture.

TO ASSEMBLE

Pour desired amount of dressing over prepared noodles and toss. Top with chopped cashews.

TOMATO, CUCUMBER, AND SWEET ONION SALAD
DINNER, DAY 16
SERVES 1

Mediterranean influenced, this dish will linger in your mind and might even inspire a trip to the sea. The dressing is so light it allows for the beautiful flavors of the vegetables to shine through. Chop it or stack it—either way it's a satisfying meal.

FOR THE TOMATO

1 large heirloom tomato, or other large red tomato

1 Persian cucumber, or if using standard cucumber, peel skin

¼ sweet onion, use more or less as desired

4 basil leaves, ribbon cut

METHOD

We've stacked this recipe, but chopping tomato, cucumber, and onion into bite-size pieces works as well. To stack, slice the tomato, cucumber, and onion into even stackable pieces. Cut basil leaves into ribbons. Place all ingredients into a large bowl.

FOR THE DRESSING

1 garlic clove, crushed

1½ tablespoons extra-virgin olive oil

1 teaspoon cider vinegar

1 drizzle maple syrup or sweetener of choice, to taste (no white sugar)

⅛ teaspoon Dijon mustard

Sea salt and pepper, to taste

METHOD

Whisk all dressing ingredients until well incorporated

TO ASSEMBLE

Pour dressing onto salad and lightly toss.

NOTE: This is a light dinner and can be followed with a dessert from pages 202–18.

TRY THIS TIP

To take the edge off raw onion, soak onion slices in equal parts cider vinegar and water and cover for 20+ minutes. Even if you enjoy raw onions, these soaked onions are delicious.

CURRIED COCONUT PASTA BOWL
DINNER, DAY 17
SERVES 1

The spice of life is what's needed to enjoy each moment. Whether it is food, companionship, career, or creativity, a little spice can be exciting. If you are looking for an exhilarating taste, then look no further than this Thai-inspired dish. The savory curry sauce will leave your mouth happy. This better-than-takeout recipe is easy to follow and has medicinal benefits, as well as flavor. You might want to introduce your family or friends to this delectable dish.

FOR THE NOODLES

1 large zucchini, or 2 small

1 pinch sea salt

Squeeze of lemon juice

METHOD

Spiralize zucchini, or use a potato or julienne peeler to make noodles. Place zucchini noodles in a bowl and sprinkle with salt and lemon juice. Lightly toss. Leave the noodles to "sweat" for 15 minutes or so while you make the curry sauce.

TRY THIS TIP

For a little crunch, chopped cashews or finely chopped carrots may be added.

½ cup cashews, soaked if possible

½–1 tablespoon coconut water

One 2-inch slice avocado

2 cherry tomatoes, seeded

1 garlic clove, peeled and chopped

½ teaspoon curry powder

1 pinch cumin

Fingernail-size piece of ginger, peeled

1 pinch turmeric

1 teaspoon coconut or extra-virgin olive oil

⅛ cup cilantro

¼ cup or small handful unsweetened coconut flakes

1–2 grinds fresh ground black pepper and sea salt

1 pinch cayenne powder, or to taste, depending on heat preference

METHOD

Place all sauce ingredients in a blender and blend until smooth. Add more coconut water if needed to make a thick, creamy smooth sauce. Taste and adjust spices to your liking.

FOR THE TOPPING

1 scallion, chopped

3 basil leaves, chopped

3–4 cilantro stems, leaves removed and rough chopped

1 small handful unsweetened coconut flakes

TO ASSEMBLE

Drain any liquid from the noodles and pat dry. Dry any liquid from the bowl and place noodles back in bowl. Add desired amount of sauce. Toss well. Place noodles in a serving bowl and sprinkle on toppings.

WARM NOODLE SOUP
DINNER, DAY 18
SERVES 1

In Asia, they like to slurp their noodle as a sign of enjoyment. In Italy, noodles are twisted up on a fork and eaten in one bite. If you take too much on the fork, allowing some to fall back into the plate, it is considered bad manners. In China, the custom is to eat long continuous noodle strips, which are symbolic of longevity. So if you wish to have a long and healthy life, leave your zucchini noodle strips long. Slurping is up to you.

FOR THE NOODLES

1 small zucchini, peeled

1 pinch sea salt

Squeeze of lemon juice

METHOD

Spiralize zucchini, or use a potato or julienne peeler to make noodles. Place zucchini noodles in a bowl and sprinkle with salt and lemon juice. Lightly toss. Leave the noodles to "sweat" for 15 minutes. Drain and pat dry.

RECIPE CONTINUES

1½ cups filtered water, warmed on the stovetop—do not overheat or boil

4 dried shiitake mushrooms, soaked in water until softened

1 tablespoon chopped sweet onion

½ celery rib, roughly chopped

½ carrot, peeled and roughly chopped

1 teaspoon tamari

1 small knob ginger, peeled

1 tablespoon organic miso or add another 1½ teaspoons of tamari,

½ teaspoon tahini or 1 tablespoon cashews

1 tablespoon fresh cilantro

1 pinch or grind black pepper

½ garlic clove

METHOD

Place warmed water and remaining broth ingredients into a blender and blend until completely smooth. Taste for seasonings and adjust if necessary. Pour the warm broth mixture into a small pot.

FOR THE VEGETABLES

½ celery stalk, thinly sliced

½ carrot, peeled and thinly sliced or shredded

3 snow peas, thinly sliced (optional)

⅛ cup thinly sliced or shredded white cabbage (optional)

METHOD

Prep vegetables and place them in a bowl.

TO ASSEMBLE

Put vegetables and noodles into the pot of warm broth and let sit to absorb and soften the veggies. If necessary, lightly warm broth again. The temperature should be just warm to the touch. Do not overheat. Place in a bowl to serve.

VEGGIE CHOP SALAD
DINNER, DAY 19
SERVES 1

You might be thinking about opening up your own wrap shop, as you are probably an expert by now at wrapping up veggies. It's such a great skill to have for quick tasty meals and snacks. This salad can be placed in romaine lettuce leaves to make a wrap, or piled on top of a large, ribbon-cut romaine leaf salad or greens of your choice.

FOR THE WRAP OR BASE

2 to 4 romaine lettuce leaves, or salad greens of choice

METHOD

Romaine leaves are best when they are cold and crisp. Wash leaves, shake the water off, and wrap in a paper towel. Place inside a plastic bag or wrap again in a clean cotton kitchen towel and chill in the refrigerator for 1 hour.

FOR THE VEGETABLE FILLING

½ large carrot

½ red bell pepper

1 tablespoon chopped shallot, or equal amount sweet onion

¼ cup broccoli florets

2 tablespoons sunflower seeds

½ celery rib, chopped

METHOD

Toss all ingredients into a food processor, except celery, and pulse into small, bite-size pieces. Place in a mixing bowl and add the chopped celery.

RECIPE CONTINUES

2–3 tablespoons cashews

1 scallion

1 small garlic clove

1 teaspoon fresh dill, or ½ teaspoon dried

2 tablespoons lemon juice

Sea salt and pepper, to taste

3 tablespoons filtered water, more or less as needed

METHOD

Toss all ingredients into a blender. As you blend, add a tablespoon of water at a time to achieve a smooth, thick, creamy dressing, stopping machine to scrape down sides. Too much water will make dressing too thin.

TO ASSEMBLE

Toss the filling and dressing together. Spoon the filling into two or more leaves and eat. Of course you can use any green leaf you like, or even place a scoop of this goodness on top of a green salad. Travels well and lasts 3 to 4 days in the refrigerator.

FILLED SWEET RED BELL PEPPER
DINNER, DAY 20
SERVES 1

Sweet bell peppers come in a variety of colors including red, yellow, orange, green, brown, white, and purple. Almost everywhere we travel, the farmers' markets have sweet red bell peppers. In Spain, Italy, and Portugal, just to name a few countries, red bell peppers can be 7 to 10 inches long. Each pepper has a slightly different taste. Red is the sweetest tasting but choose any color pepper you like. This dish is simply gorgeous.

FOR THE PEPPER

1 sweet bell pepper

METHOD

Cut pepper in half and remove all white parts and seeds with a paring knife.

FOR THE FILLING

½ red or yellow bell pepper, small diced

4-inch piece cucumber, peeled and seeded

½ tomato, seeded and small diced

1 scallion, chopped

1 tablespoon corn

½ celery rib, small diced

A few basil leaves, chopped or ribbon cut

1 romaine lettuce leaf, small and ribbon cut

METHOD

Prep vegetables and toss together in a small bowl.

1 teaspoon lemon juice

1 tablespoon extra-virgin olive oil

1 tablespoon chopped walnuts

Sea salt and pepper, to taste

METHOD

Whisk together all of the ingredients. Taste and adjust salt and pepper if necessary.

TO ASSEMBLE

Toss the filling and dressing together. Place halved peppers on a plate
and spoon in filling.

KALE SHREDS WITH CASHEW RANCH
DINNER, DAY 21

SERVES 1

We end this final week with a tasty salad that will keep you addicted to kale, possibly forever. Kale is such an important green to add to your weekly meals. There are many ways to consume this dark leafy green including smoothies, wraps, and salads. We are sure you are going to love this version of kale salad.

FOR THE SALAD

2 cups kale leaves, stems removed and finely shredded

2–3 teaspoons extra-virgin olive oil

1 pinch sea salt

½ corn on the cob, kernels removed, or ⅔ cup frozen corn

1 Persian cucumber or ½ cup English cucumber, small diced

METHOD

Stack 4 to 5 de-stemmed kale leaf halves on top of each other. Roll up tightly and ribbon cut into thin slices. Continue until you have 2 or more cups. Place into a bowl and pour on olive oil and salt. Massage lightly with your hands to soften the kale shreds. When they are just slightly wilted, add corn and cucumber and lightly toss together.

FOR THE DRESSING

¼ cup cashew pieces

1 teaspoon extra-virgin olive oil

2 teaspoons lemon juice

Sea salt and pepper, to taste

¼ teaspoon onion powder

¼ teaspoon garlic powder

¼ cup filtered water

Place all ingredients into a blender and blend until everything is combined. The dressing might not be completely smooth, but that is normal.

TO ASSEMBLE

Pour desired amount of dressing onto the salad and toss.

TRY THIS TIP

This is a good salad to add some sauerkraut or kimchi to.

ON-THE-GO SIMPLE SMOOTHIES

Red High Energy, Heart Healing

Orange Adventure, Immunity Boosting

Yellow Illuminating, Anti-Inflammatory

Detoxifying Green Lemonade

Blue Calming, Longevity

Indigo Intuition

Violet Inspiration

Pink Nurturing

White Creative

Quick and Delicious

A Rainbow of Colors

When we see rainbows, we tend to believe it's a lucky sign. Rainbows appear in seven colors, so it's appropriate we have seven smoothies for good luck—and health, of course.

For our 21-Day Plan, we have chosen to make smoothies instead of juices because most people own blenders. The other reason we chose smoothies is they take less time to make and, because of the added fiber, they can be more filling. If you prefer juicing, feel free to use the following recipes with little adjustments to make a juice.

Smoothies are quick to make, but not everyone has the luxury of time to make a smoothie every morning. If you are one of those people, you can make a batch of smoothies over the weekend and freeze them for the week ahead. Having smoothies ready to go in the freezer can make life much easier and assure you are getting the nutrients you need. In case you're wondering if they will lose their nutrients, the answer is not enough to worry about. Freezable containers are a great investment or use glass mason jars with tight-fitting lids. In order to safely freeze your weekly smoothies, all you need to do is pour your smoothie into the freezable container or jar and leave 1½ inches at the top for expansion. If you need to grab and go in the morning, remove the smoothie from the freezer the night prior and put it in the refrigerator to thaw overnight. If you are not going to drink it in the morning but plan to drink it later in the day, remove it from the freezer in the morning and take it along with you. Refrigerate at work if possible. Alternatively, if you have time, all weekly smoothie ingredients can be washed at once and frozen in a zip-lock freezer bag for the week. In the morning when you are ready to make your smoothie, all you do is put the frozen ingredients into your blender, add desired liquid, and blend. A third choice, if you are making your smoothies daily, is to freeze all the fruit and add fresh greens to the morning smoothie before blending. The frozen fruit will help make your smoothies thick and cold. Some of the big box stores and health food stores carry organic frozen fruit, which can be a time saver in fixing smoothies.

If you make all your smoothies at one time, your blender only needs to be thoroughly cleaned once, with only a quick rinse in between smoothies. You may also want to make half your smoothies at one time and the other half during the week when you have more time.

These smoothies will help you get your daily requirement of fruits.

TRY THIS TIP
Add a handful of greens to any smoothie.

RED HIGH ENERGY, HEART HEALING

SERVES 1

INGREDIENTS

1 cup almond milk (see page 53)

¼ beet, peeled and cut into chunks

½ cup raspberries

½ cup strawberries

1 teaspoon pure vanilla extract

2 Medjool dates

METHOD

Place all ingredients in a blender and blend until smooth. If not freezing ahead, add 4 to 5 ice cubes and blend again. Ready to drink!

ORANGE ADVENTURE, IMMUNITY BOOSTING

SERVES 1

INGREDIENTS

2 oranges, peeled and seeded

½ cup almond milk (see page 53)

1 teaspoon pure vanilla extract

1 carrot, cut into small chunks

1 summer stone fruit—peach, plumb, nectarine, or fruit of choice

METHOD

Place all ingredients in a blender and blend until smooth. If not freezing ahead, add 4 to 5 ice cubes and blend again. Ready to drink!

YELLOW ILLUMINATING, ANTI-INFLAMMATORY

SERVES 1

INGREDIENTS

½ cup coconut water

1 cup pineapple

½ Granny Smith apple

1 orange

½ banana

1 teaspoon pure vanilla extract

METHOD

Place all ingredients in a blender and blend until smooth. If not freezing ahead, add 4 to 5 ice cubes and blend again. Ready to drink!

DETOXIFYING GREEN LEMONADE

SERVES 1

INGREDIENTS

1 cup green tea, cooled

1 medium Persian cucumber, peeled, or ½ standard cucumber, peeled

½ Granny Smith apple

½ cup spinach

1 tablespoon fresh Italian parsley or cilantro

½ lemon, peeled and seeded

1 Medjool date

METHOD

Place all ingredients in a blender and blend until smooth. If not freezing ahead, add 4 to 5 ice cubes and blend again. Ready to drink!

BLUE CALMING, LONGEVITY

SERVES 1

INGREDIENTS

½ cup strawberries

½ cup dark leafy greens

½ cup blueberries

1 cup filtered water

2 Medjool dates

METHOD

Place all ingredients in a blender and blend until smooth. If not freezing ahead, add 4 to 5 ice cubes and blend again. Ready to drink!

INDIGO INTUITION

SERVES 1

INGREDIENTS

1 cup blackberries

1 cup dark leafy greens

2 Medjool dates

1 cup green tea, cooled

METHOD

Place all ingredients in a blender and blend until smooth. If not freezing ahead, add 4 to 5 ice cubes and blend again. Ready to drink!

VIOLET INSPIRATION

SERVES 1

INGREDIENTS

1 cup almond milk (see page 53)

1 teaspoon pure vanilla extract

1 cup blueberries

2 Medjool dates

METHOD

Place all ingredients in a blender and blend until smooth. If not freezing ahead, add 4 to 5 ice cubes and blend again. Ready to drink!

PINK NURTURING

SERVES 1

INGREDIENTS

1 cup watermelon

6 strawberries

2 sprigs mint

¼–½ cup filter water

METHOD

Place all ingredients in a blender and blend until smooth. If not freezing ahead, add 4 to 5 ice cubes and blend again. Ready to drink!

WHITE CREATIVE

SERVES 1

INGREDIENTS

1 small handful cashews

1 ¼ cups filtered water

1 teaspoon pure vanilla extract

4–5 Medjool dates

⅛ teaspoon cardamom or cinnamon

METHOD

Place all ingredients in a blender and blend until smooth. If not freezing ahead, add 4 to 5 ice cubes and blend again. Ready to drink!

QUICK AND DELICIOUS

SERVES 1

INGREDIENTS

1 small handful cashews

4–5 Medjool dates

½ teaspoon turmeric powder or small nub fresh ginger, peeled

½ banana

1½ cups filtered water

METHOD

Place all ingredients in a blender and blend until smooth. Add 4–5 ice cubes and blend again. Ready to drink!

SNACKS

Raw Macaroons

Fresh Fruit Delight

Crisp Apple Slices with Almond Butter

Cacao Shake

Banana Almond Butter Sushi

Fresh Stone Fruit or Fruit in Season

Tomato Veggie Stack

Naked One-Minute Avocado

Nut Butter Green Leaf

Frozen Grapes

Fruits and Vegetables

RAW MACAROONS

MAKES 10-12 MACAROONS

INGREDIENTS

½ cup almonds

1 cup unsweetened coconut flakes

2 tablespoons maple syrup

2 tablespoons coconut oil

1 teaspoon pure vanilla extract

METHOD

Place almonds in blender and grind into flour. You will have more than ½ cup when ground, which you will use most of—set aside the rest, as it will be incorporated in a moment. Place coconut flakes, maple syrup, coconut oil, ½ cup almond flour, and vanilla ingredients in a food processor. Pulse until well combined. Scrape mixture into a bowl and add ¼ cup almond flour and 1 small handful coconut flakes and blend in with a fork. Take about 1 teaspoon of the mixture into your hand and press together lightly, then roll into a ball in the palms of your hands. Place balls on a baking sheet covered with parchment paper. Press balls down slightly to flatten bottom, but leaving a rounded shape on the top. See photo on page 190.

TRY THIS TIP

To make chocolate macaroons, add 1 tablespoon cacao powder when mixing in food processor. Refrigerate covered, or freeze.

FRESH FRUIT DELIGHT

SERVES 1

INGREDIENTS

1 orange

1 banana

½ cup berries of choice

1 tablespoon chopped almonds or walnuts

Sprinkle of cinnamon

METHOD

Peel orange and cut into bite-size pieces. Peel banana and cut into bite-size pieces. Place fruit in a bowl with the berries and sprinkle with chopped nuts and cinnamon.

TRY THIS TIP

Choose any three fruits in season for a great snack.

CRISP APPLE SLICES WITH ALMOND BUTTER

SERVES 1

INGREDIENTS

1 Granny Smith apple, chilled

2 tablespoons almond butter

Sprinkle of cinnamon, for topping

METHOD

Cut apple in half and remove seeds and center core. Slice apple medium thin. Arrange like a fan on a small plate and scoop almond butter in the middle. A little sprinkle of cinnamon adds extra health goodness. Use a small butter knife and spread almond butter on one slice at a time as you eat them. We like this method as it makes you slow down while eating and makes this treat last longer.

BANANA ALMOND BUTTER SUSHI

SERVES 1

INGREDIENTS

2 tablespoons almond butter

1–2 bananas

Sprinkle of sunflower seeds,
hemp seeds, Cinnamon, or cardamom,
for topping

METHOD

If you keep your nut butters in the refrigerator, remove for about 1 hour before using for this recipe. Spread softened almond butter to cover the top of the banana. Sprinkle seeds, cinnamon, or cardamom on top. Place on waxed paper and freeze for 10–15 minutes. Remove from freezer and cut into chunks. Eat with chopsticks.

CACAO SHAKE

SERVES 1

INGREDIENTS

1 cup almond or cashew milk, or
3 tablespoons hemp seeds and
1 cup filtered water

2–3 tablespoons cacao powder,
depending on richness preference

1 teaspoon pure vanilla extract

1 tablespoon maple syrup or sweetener
of choice (no white sugar), to taste

3–4 ice cubes

Sprinkle of hemp seeds, cardamom, or
cinnamon, for topping

METHOD

Place all ingredients, except ice cubes and topping options, in a blender and blend until very smooth. Add ice and blend again. Top with a sprinkle of hemp seeds, cardamom, or cinnamon. Pour in glass, cup, or wine glass.

FRESH STONE FRUIT OR FRUIT IN SEASON

SERVES 1

Eating fruit in its natural state is so delicious, sometimes we forget that Mother Nature thought of it all. She put together just the right amount of sweet or tart and a great variety of amazing textures. Here are some of our favorite stand-alone fruits. Stone fruits arrive in summer, so we like to consume as many varieties as possible. Of course, you can always combine any fruits. Melons should be eaten alone for best digestion. On our list, we mention some our favorite and more exotic types of fruit, but don't leave off some of the common favorites as well.

STONE FRUITS

Peaches, Nectarines, Apricots, and Plums

TROPICAL FRUITS

Papaya, Mango, and Pineapple

OTHER FRUITS

Cherimoyas, Kiwis, and Melons

TOMATO VEGGIE STACK

SERVES 1

INGREDIENTS

1 thick slice large heirloom tomato, or other large variety

2 slices avocado

Spinach

Basil leaves

Shredded carrot

Extra-virgin olive oil, to taste

Sea salt and pepper, to taste

METHOD

Stack all ingredients onto a plate or bowl. Drizzle on olive oil, salt, and pepper. See photo on page 32.

NAKED ONE-MINUTE AVOCADO

SERVES 1

INGREDIENTS

1 ripe avocado

Sea salt and pepper, or leftover salad dressing or vegan mayo, to taste

METHOD

Cut avocado in half and remove seed. Sprinkle on salt and pepper, dressing, or vegan mayo and eat with a spoon.

NUT BUTTER GREEN LEAF

SERVES 1

INGREDIENTS

1-3 tablespoons almond butter

Collard or romaine lettuce leaves

1 teaspoon sunflower seeds

Sprouts (optional)

METHOD

Spread almond butter on desired leaf and sprinkle on the sunflower seeds and optional sprouts. Fold leaf over and eat.

FROZEN GRAPES

In case you haven't tried this before, wash grapes and pat them dry. Place them into a zip-lock freezer bag and freeze overnight. Eat as desired for a snack, dessert, or just anytime because they are so delicious.

FRUITS AND VEGETABLES

Two of the easiest fast foods to grab when you are hungry are fruits and veggies. If you are in a hurry and can't take time to fix a proper meal, we suggest you grab a fruit or two or some veggies. This will hold you over until you have time to fix a more substantial meal.

you are going to have a super sensational day.

GUILT-FREE DESSERTS

Chocolate Pudding

Banana Cacao Smoothie

Chocolate Almond/Peanut Butter Cups

Cacao Caramel Cupcakes

Coconut Chocolate Truffles

Carrot-Orange-Lemon Cake

Apple Caramel Tart

Banana Blueberry Bites

Strawberry Banana Ice Cream

Banana Cinnamon Ice Cream

NOTE: All desserts make more than one serving. You can freeze any dessert, making it convenient to have a sweet or two throughout the week—unless your family makes them all disappear.

CHOCOLATE PUDDING

SERVES 4

This is a truly memorable and simple dessert. If you serve this dish to others, don't let them know beforehand that the creamy pudding-like texture is made with Hass avocados. For some reason, some folks can't imagine avocados in a dessert. But one taste and minds will be changed. Yes, any avocado will work, but we like to use Hass as they are the most buttery of all avocados. If you are interested in making a pie some day, you can make a nut crust similar to the Cacao Carmel Cupcakes and fill it with this Chocolate Pudding. Chocolate Pudding is so quick to make and so satisfying this might become a staple in your refrigerator.

INGREDIENTS

2 large Hass avocados, ripe but not over ripe

4 tablespoons cacao powder

2 teaspoons pure vanilla extract

2 tablespoons coconut oil

3 tablespoons maple syrup, or more to taste

1–2 pinches sea salt (optional)

METHOD

Cut avocados in half and remove seeds. Scrape or squeeze avocado from its shell into a blender or food processor. Add cacao powder, vanilla, and coconut oil. Use the tamper from the blender to keep mixture moving, if available. When smooth, scrape into a dish and refrigerate for an hour or more, or eat immediately.

TRY THIS TIP

Add 2 to 3 teaspoons orange juice and 1 teaspoon orange zest. Top with a slice of orange with rind removed, or garnish with raspberries.

BANANA CACAO SMOOTHIE

SERVES 1

Yes, this is a dessert. It's also a feel-good, satisfying, I-want-this-for-dinner kind of meal. It's decadent and somehow boosts your mood. If you feel a craving coming on, you can be satisfied in just minutes with this Banana Cacao Smoothie. Who say's you can't have this for breakfast? Not us!

INGREDIENTS

½ banana

1–2 tablespoons cacao powder, depending on how chocolatey you like it

1 small handful cashews

2 Medjool dates

1 splash pure vanilla extract

1¼ cups filtered water

4 ice cubes

METHOD

Place all ingredients, except ice cubes, into a food processor and blend until smooth. Add ice cubes and blend again.

CHOCOLATE ALMOND/PEANUT BUTTER CUPS

MAKES 6 CUPS

Remember Reese's Peanut Butter Cups? Well, life just got better. Yes, these are better in every way. They are made with dark raw cacao powder, coconut oil, and seeds, lightly sweetened—they are essentially healthy. We call this one our favorite go-to-freezer desserts. Eat soon after removing from the freezer as they melt quickly.

INGREDIENTS

2 teaspoons hemp seeds

2 teaspoons sunflower seeds

2 teaspoons pumpkin seeds

2 tablespoons each almond and peanut butter

7 tablespoons solid coconut oil, melted

7 tablespoons cacao powder

3 tablespoons + 1 teaspoon maple syrup

METHOD

Mix seeds together in a bowl and set aside. Place solid coconut oil in a bowl and place over a pan of hot water to melt. Mix almond and peanut butters together in a bowl and place over a pan of hot water to soften. Place melted coconut oil, cacao powder, and maple syrup in a bowl and combine well. Keep mixing until all granules of cacao powder are well incorporated and smooth. Taste for sweetness and add more maple syrup, if desired.

TO ASSEMBLE

Place paper cupcake holders into cupcake tins. Put 4 teaspoons of chocolate into the bottom of paper cups. Drop 1 teaspoon nut butter mixture on top of the chocolate. Sprinkle 1 teaspoon combined seeds on top of nut butter. Lightly tap tin on kitchen counter to settle ingredients. Top each cup with 1 tablespoon of chocolate and divide the remaining chocolate between the six cups. Lightly tap down tin when finished to meld together. Place in freezer covered with plastic wrap. Eat right from the freezer, as coconut oil softens quickly at room temperature.

CACAO CARAMEL CUPCAKES

MAKES 12 CUPCAKES

NOTE: Cashew pieces and Medjool dates need to be soaked. See the directions in the For the Caramel Layer section that follows.

One bite of this dessert and it feels like you are eating chocolate candy. But in fact, these cupcakes are like mini tarts with a thin crust on the bottom. If you are a fan of salted caramel, feel free to put a pinch of sea salt in with the caramel layer or on top of the finished cacao layer. The first bite of this creamy dessert will make all things right again.

FOR THE BOTTOM CRUST

½ cup walnuts

½ cup cashews

½ cup Medjool dates

METHOD

Place nuts in food processor and pulse into smallish pieces. Add the dates and pulse to incorporate dates. Pinch the mixture in your fingers to see if it sticks together. Put cupcake papers into baking cupcake tins. Press 1 tablespoon of crust into bottom of each cupcake paper. Refrigerate until caramel layer is ready to spread.

FOR THE CARAMEL LAYER

1 cup cashew pieces, soaked for 3–4 hours

½ cup Medjool dates, soaked for 20 minutes, or ¼ cup maple syrup

1 teaspoon pure vanilla extract

4 tablespoons coconut oil

2 tablespoons cacao powder

3 tablespoons filtered water

Place all ingredients in a food processor. Blend until smooth, adding water a tablespoon at a time. Use as little water as possible. Remove tin from refrigerator and spread 1 tablespoon caramel layer over each nut crust and place tin back in refrigerator.

FOR THE CACAO LAYER

9 tablespoons solid coconut oil, melted

9 level tablespoons cacao powder (or less if you're not a chocoholic)

5 tablespoons maple syrup

METHOD

Place solid coconut oil in a bowl and place over a pan of hot water to melt. Whisk all ingredients in a bowl until completely smooth.

TO ASSEMBLE

Remove cupcake tin from refrigerator and place 1 tablespoon of cacao mixture on top of caramel layer. Divide any leftover cacao between the cupcakes. Place back into refrigerator and leave overnight. Wrap in individual plastic wrap and freeze.

TRY THIS TIP

Add a splash of orange juice and zest to the caramel layer.

COCONUT CHOCOLATE TRUFFLES

MAKES 22 TRUFFLES

You can tell by now, we love chocolate. It's a superfood and so healthy and it just tastes so satisfying. This is one of the easiest recipes and it packs a big punch when it comes to a sweet craving. Pass these babies around at work and you will be a hit at the office. This is also one of those recipes that you can get creative with: add a little cardamom, cinnamon, or pumpkin spice around the holidays, it up to you! It's okay if you eat one while rolling them into balls, and then refrigerate the rest. Who's counting, right?

INGREDIENTS

1 cup pecans or walnuts, or a combination of both

½ cup finely shredded coconut

5 tablespoons cacao powder

1 tablespoon pure vanilla extract

¼ cup + 1 tablespoon coconut oil

2 cup Medjool dates, pits removed

1 tablespoon almond butter

Shredded coconut, cacao powder, ground/crushed nuts, hemp seeds, or matcha powder, or a combination of any, for topping

METHOD

Place all ingredients, except the suggested toppings, into a food processor and chop until well combined. Remove blade from the processor and take a spoonful of the mixture into your hand and roll into bite-size balls. Place onto wax or parchment paper. Store in an airtight container in the refrigerator.

TO ASSEMBLE

Pour desired toppings into a small plate and roll the truffle into the mix. Keep refrigerated or freeze, as coconut oil softens quickly.

CARROT-ORANGE-LEMON CAKE

MAKES 4 RAMEKINS

NOTE: Medjool dates and cashews need to be soaked. See the directions for the dates in the For the Muffin Base section below, and for the cashews in the For the Frosting section.

What we love about this recipe is the sweetness of the carrots and the tartness of the citrus blended together. Top it off with lemon cashew cream frosting and you will have to conclude that desserts can be healthy and delicious at the same time.

FOR THE MUFFIN BASE

1½ cups roughly shredded carrots

Zest and juice of 1 lemon

Zest and juice of 1 orange

½ cup walnuts

½ cup Medjool dates, soaked for 15–20 minutes

1 tablespoon pure vanilla extract

⅛ teaspoon cinnamon or pumpkin spice

1 pinch sea salt

METHOD

Shred carrots with attachment of a food processor or a box grater. Zest lemon and orange and squeeze juice from half of each. Place carrots, lemon, orange, and remaining ingredients in a food processor and pulse until combined. Divide into 4 small ramekins using 4 tablespoons each.

1 cup cashews, soaked for 2–4 hours

1 tablespoon pure vanilla extract

1½ tablespoons coconut oil

1 tablespoon maple syrup

Juice of 1 lemon

Filtered water as needed

Cinnamon for sprinkling

METHOD

Place frosting ingredients into a blender. Add 2 tablespoons water and blend. Scrape down sides and add more water to make a very thick, smooth texture.

TO ASSEMBLE

Frost cakes and sprinkle with cinnamon. Store covered in refrigerator.

APPLE CARAMEL TART

MAKES 1 TART AND SERVES 3-4

Layering is the key to this classic-gone-wild dessert. An apple tart is an undeniable classic and the caramel layer makes this dessert wildly delicious. Our tart is made in a 4-inch tart pan with removable bottom, but if you don't have one, simply line a small container with plastic wrap and proceed as directed. When your tart is chilled, sit down with your favorite tea and have a slice. It's so good, you just might have to have a second serving.

FOR THE CRUST

½ cup almonds

⅓ cup Medjool dates

1 teaspoon pure vanilla extract

METHOD

Place almonds in a food processor and pulse into small pieces. Add dates and vanilla and pulse until mixture sticks together when pinched between your fingers. Add a drop of water if necessary for mixture to stick together. Press crust into 4-inch tart pan with removable bottom, or a small pan lined with plastic wrap.

FOR THE FILLING

1 heaping tablespoon almond butter

1 splash pure vanilla extract

1 tablespoon maple syrup

1 teaspoon liquid coconut oil

½ teaspoon lemon juice

1 large apple, peeled and small diced

METHOD

Place all ingredients but the apple into a mixing bowl and whisk together until very smooth. Place diced apple into the bowl and toss to coat. Remove tart pan from the freezer and spoon in the filling.

2 teaspoons liquid coconut oil

2 teaspoons maple syrup

⅛ teaspoon lemon juice

⅛ teaspoon pure vanilla extract

METHOD

Whisk together until smooth.

TO ASSEMBLE

Spoon caramel mixture on top of refrigerated tart. Garnish with thinly sliced apples and cover with plastic wrap and refrigerate.

BANANA BLUEBERRY BITES

MAKES 8 SQUARES

With just 2 ingredients, this recipe couldn't be easier. We use blueberries, but mangos would work as well. You can use common ice cube trays or silicone trays of different shapes. These frozen goodies can also be dropped into a glass to chill a smoothie. Eating Banana Blueberry Bites can make you feel like a child again.

INGREDIENTS

2 ripe bananas

½ cup blueberries, or more if desired

METHOD

Place bananas and blueberries in a food processor and process until smooth. Spoon into ice cube trays. Freeze until solid. When frozen solid, pop them out and store in plastic zip-lock bags. Best eaten frozen. Can also be used in smoothies

STRAWBERRY BANANA ICE CREAM

SERVES 1

There's nothing better than sweet, ripe, red strawberries in season. We highly suggest you only buy organic strawberries, since non-organic varieties are known to hold more pesticides than any fruit or vegetable. Presently strawberries can be purchased all year round, but we suggest buying frozen rather than fresh if they are not in season. This Strawberry Banana Ice Cream just never stops giving pleasure. There is something so comforting about a meeting between strawberries and bananas, it's like they were meant to be together. If you have fresh strawberries, cut up a few to put on top. See photo on page 203.

INGREDIENTS

1 frozen banana

½ cup frozen strawberries

1–2 tablespoons maple syrup, to taste

METHOD

If you have a juicer, use the homogenizing blade to run the frozen fruit through and stir in sweetener. Alternatively, cut bananas into small chunks and cut strawberries in half if they are large prior to freezing. Place frozen fruit ingredients into a food processor—add a couple tablespoons of water if necessary. Pulse until creamy and smooth and add sweetener.

laughter keeps you young.

BANANA CINNAMON ICE CREAM

SERVES 1

What a treat to eat ice cream and know it's nutritious. The other amazing thing about this recipe is that it's very quick to make, assuming you've previously frozen the ripe bananas. This ice cream is a soft-serve type, so if you prefer a firmer texture just place it in the freezer for about 1 hour. If you would like to serve the ice cream with a little chocolate syrup on top, whisk a tablespoon of soft or melted coconut oil with 2 teaspoons of cacao powder and 2 teaspoons of maple syrup and blend until smooth. Drizzle syrup on top of the ice cream for a banana chocolate sundae. See photo on page 203.

INGREDIENTS

1–2 frozen bananas

1 tablespoon chopped nuts

Sprinkle of cinnamon

METHOD

If you have a juicer, run frozen banana through blank screen or cut frozen bananas into small pieces and place in food processor. A slight bit of nut milk or filtered water might be needed to cream bananas. Place in a bowl and sprinkle with cinnamon and chopped nuts.

TRY THIS TIP

Add ½ teaspoon or more cacao powder for chocolate banana ice cream.

AFTERWORD

There is only one person who can do something about your health and that is you. Please take into consideration that a few healthy habits can go a long way. Create routines that will stick with you. They will only work if they are doable and realistic for you personally. If you want to eat raw foods 60 percent and cooked foods 40 percent, then so be it. If you want to relax on weekends and eat your favorite foods, fine; however, we implore you to stay away from processed foods and fast food, as these are known to take away your good health more quickly than you realize. Find foods you loved on our plan and incorporate them into your weekly menu. Eat real food, exercise, and think positive—life will support your decision. Take one step forward and the magic of good health will take one hundred steps toward you. Good health is a lifelong venture. Try to have a balanced life and alleviate stress. Keep moving in the right direction and never get discouraged. There are hundreds of thousands of us working on keeping ourselves healthy and happy—you are not alone. We wish you great health and happiness.

Check out our Raw-Vitalize YouTube channel for quick tips and demonstrations on some of the recipes in this book. You can get in contact with us via our email address, Raw.Vitalize@yahoo.com.

–MIMI KIRK AND MIA KIRK WHITE

ACKNOWLEDGMENTS

What is a food-oriented book without photos? Not much! A really big thank you to Mike Mendell for all the beautiful and creative photography. You are one patient and talented man—it's always a pleasure working with you. Thanks to our very close and supportive immediate family—we love you all very much. We are listing in alphabetical order, as we know some of you like to play "I'm the favorite" game. Audrey, Dan, Gigi, Gunner, Hannah, Jonas, Karly, Lisa, Luke, Mackenzie, and Rocky. Thanks to my big sister and Mia's aunt, Arlene, who always protects us and thinks we are perfect. We are grateful to our clients and social media friends for all the support they have provided us over the years. Kari Stuart from ICM Partners and Ann Treistman from The Countryman Press—you are both such great people to work with: creative, honest, and smart. We both have great long- and short-time friends who are interesting, fun to be with and always there for us. We are naming just a few, but there are so many more and we thank you as well.

Mimi's friends: Thanks to my long-time bestie Julie Kavner, and to my wonderful friend Robin Leach. Special thanks to my circle of friends including Susan Santilena of The Real Kitchen Coach; Chef Jean-Christian Jury, Eileen Chousa Katzenstein, Michael Keller, Catrinel Popescu of Do Good Academy; Miriam and Jens from Villa Vegana, Mallorca; Patricia St Clair, and her team at Port Amore–Puerto d' Andratx; Mallorca; Victoria Davis of Nourishment Now; and Christine Mayr of Crua Gourmet Cuisine.

Mia's friends: A special thanks to Mary White and to my sisterhood: Emily Dodge, Clarissa Kussin, Gina Chapman, Dorothy Holland, Kim Faillon, Cindy Maynard, Paula Detyens, JoEllen Constine, Susan Brown, Denyelle Mehfoud, Sharon Smith, Erin Sammons, Sonya Pusey, Sarah Rawlings, Laura Olinger, Denise Grega, Jennifer Little, Nicole Elliott, and Nicole Arruda, as well as all the other people in my life who helped me to be fearless and authentic.

INDEX

21-day plan, 41–45

almond butter
Apple Caramel Tart, 212–13
Apple Sunrise, 55
Banana Almond Butter Sushi, 193
Banana Pudding, 77
Banana Smoothie Bowl, 66
Buddha Bowl, 132–33
Coconut Chocolate Truffles, 208
Crisp Apple Slices with Almond Butter, 191
Fruit Smoothie Bowl, 68
Nut Butter, Banana, and Veggie Collard Wrap, 122–23
Nut Butter Green Leaf, 197
Nut Seed and Fruit Bowl, 73
Pad Thai, 163–65
Sweet Potato Swirls, 80–81
almond milk, 51
almonds
Apple Caramel Tart, 212–13
Chia Seed Cranberry Oat Bar, 61
Fresh Fruit Delight, 191
Nut Seed and Fruit Bowl, 73
Quick Granola and Almond Milk, 58
Raw Macaroons, 190
Stuffed Tomato, 108–9
apples
Apple, Purple Cabbage, and Beet Salad, 120–21
Apple Caramel Tart, 212–13
Apple Sunrise, 55
Banana Smoothie Bowl, 66
Creamy Thai Soup, 92–93
Crisp Apple Slices with Almond Butter, 191
Detox Glow Salad, 86–88
Detoxifying Green Lemonade, 184
Fruit Smoothie Bowl, 68
Nut Seed and Fruit Bowl, 73
SuperFruit Bowl, 57
Vitality Soup, 152–53
Yellow Illuminating smoothie, 184
Arrabbiata Checca sauce, 158
Asian sauce, 125
avocados
Avocado Vessel, 112–13
Buddha Bowl, 132–33
Chocolate Pudding, 202
Chop Chop Hooray, 100–101
Collard Rollups, 157
Curried Coconut Pasta Bowl, 168–69
Detox Glow Salad, 86–88
Friends of the Nori Roll, 103–4
Guacamole with Veggie Sticks, 148–49
Naked One-Minute Avocado, 197
Nut Butter, Banana, and Veggie Collard Wrap, 122–23
Oh So Good Simple Sandwich, 119
Street Taco, 110–11
Super Amazing Heirloom Tomato Salad, 82–83
Sweet Corn Chowder, 151
Tapas Salad, 89–91
Tomato Veggie Stack, 194
Vitality Soup, 152–53
Warm Curried Cream of Carrot Soup, 146
Warm Spicy/Mild Chili, 160–62
Awaken drink, 34–35

bananas
Banana Almond Butter Sushi, 193
Banana Blueberry Bites, 214
Banana Cacao Smoothie, 203
Banana Cinnamon Ice Cream, 216
Banana Pudding, 77
Banana Smoothie Bowl, 66
Banana Vanilla Smoothie, 74
Breakfast Pudding, 60
Fresh Fruit Delight, 191
Fruit Smoothie Bowl, 68
Green Detox Smoothie, 63
Mono Fruit, 69
Nut Butter, Banana, and Veggie Collard Wrap, 122–23
Quick and Delicious smoothie, 187
Strawberry Banana Ice Cream, 215
Tropical Paradise with Cashew Cream, 52–53
Yellow Illuminating smoothie, 184
Barbecue sauce, 118
basil pesto, 138
beets
Apple, Purple Cabbage, and Beet Salad, 120
Detox Glow Salad, 86–88
Nut Butter, Banana, and Veggie Collard Wrap, 122–23
Red High Energy smoothie, 183
berries. See specific berries
blueberries
Banana Blueberry Bites, 214
Blue Calming smoothie, 185
SuperFruit Bowl, 57
Violet Inspiration smoothie, 186

Breakfast Pudding, 60
Buddha Bowl, 132–33

cacao
    Banana Cacao Smoothie, 203
    Cacao Caramel Cupcakes, 206–7
    Cacao Shake, 193
    Chocolate Almond/Peanut Butter Cups,
        204
    Chocolate Chia Seed Overnight Pudding, 70
    Chocolate Pudding, 202
    Coconut Chocolate Truffles, 208
cakes and cupcakes
    Cacao Caramel Cupcakes, 206–7
    Carrot-Orange-Lemon Cake, 210
cashew cream, in Tropical Paradise with Cashew
        Cream, 52–53
cashews
    Banana Cacao Smoothie, 203
    Banana Vanilla Smoothie, 74
    Breakfast Pudding, 60
    Buddha Bowl, 132–33
    Cacao Caramel Cupcakes, 206
    Cacao Shake, 193
    Carrot-Orange-Lemon Cake, 210–11
    Cashew Sour Cream, 110
    Cheezy Noodles, 139–140
    Chia Seed Cranberry Oat Bar, 61
    Chopped Thai Salad, 105–6
    Curried Coconut Pasta Bowl, 168–69
    Kale Shreds with Cashew Ranch, 178–79
    Mango Pudding, 64
    Nut Seed and Fruit Bowl, 73
    Pad Thai, 163–65
    Parmesan Nut Cheese, 99
    Quick and Delicious smoothie, 187
    Street Taco, 110–11
    Sweet Corn Chowder, 151
    Vegan Mayonnaise, 109
    Veggie Chop Salad, 173–75
    Warm Curried Cream of Carrot Soup, 146
    Warm Noodle Soup, 170–72
    White Creative smoothie, 187
Cheezy Noodles, 139–140
cherries
    Apple Sunrise, 55
    Chia Seed Cranberry Oat Bar, 61
chia seeds
    Breakfast Pudding, 60
    Chia Pudding, 50
    Chia Seed Cranberry Oat Bar, 61
    Chocolate Chia Seed Overnight Pudding, 70
chocolate
    Chocolate Almond/Peanut Butter Cups, 204
    Chocolate Chia Seed Overnight Pudding, 70
    Chocolate Pudding, 202
    Coconut Chocolate Truffles, 208
Chop Chop Hooray, 100–101

Chopped Thai Salad, 105–6
coconut
    Chocolate Chia Seed Overnight Pudding, 70
    Coconut Chocolate Truffles, 208
    Creamy Thai Soup, 92–93
    Curried Coconut Pasta Bowl, 168–69
    Raw Macaroons, 190
    Warm Curried Cream of Carrot Soup, 146
collards
    Collard Rollups, 157
    Nut Butter, Banana, and Veggie Collard Wrap,
        122–23
Creamy Thai Soup, 92–93
Crisp Apple Slices with Almond Butter, 191
cupcakes
    . See cakes and cupcakes
Curried Coconut Pasta Bowl, 168–69

dates. See Medjool dates
Detox Glow Salad, 86–88
Detoxifying Green Lemonade, 184
digestion, 24–25

equipment, 28
exercise, 25

Filled Sweet Red Bell Pepper, 176–77
flaxseeds
    Apple Sunrise, 55
    Banana Smoothie Bowl, 66
    SuperFruit Bowl, 57
Friends of the Nori Roll, 103–4
fruits
    Fresh Fruit Delight, 191
    Fresh Stone Fruit, 194
    Frozen Grapes, 198
    Fruit in Season, 194
    Fruits and Vegetables, 198
    Fruit Smoothie Bowl, 68
    Mono Fruit, 69
    . See also smoothies; individual fruits

ginger
    Chopped Thai Salad, 105–6
    Creamy Thai Soup, 92–93
    Curried Coconut Pasta Bowl, 168–69
    Noodle Combo with Asian Sauce, 125–26
    Pad Thai, 163–65
    Quick and Delicious smoothie, 187
    Sweet Potato Swirls, 80–81
    Warm Curried Cream of Carrot Soup, 146
    Warm Noodle Soup, 170–72
goji berries
    Apple Sunrise, 55
    Goji Berries and Oats, 76
grapefruits, in SuperFruit Bowl, 57
Green Detox Smoothie, 63
Guacamole with Veggie Sticks, 148–49

Hardy Harvest, 54
hemp seeds
    Banana Almond Butter Sushi, 193
    Buddha Bowl, 132–33
    Cacao Shake, 193
    Chocolate Almond/Peanut Butter Cups, 204
    Coconut Chocolate Truffles, 208
    Goji Berries and Oats, 76
    Green Detox Smoothie, 63
    Hardy Harvest, 54
    Nut Seed and Fruit Bowl, 73
    Quick Granola and Almond Milk, 58
hydration, 27

ice cream
    Banana Cinnamon Ice Cream, 216
    Strawberry Banana Ice Cream, 215
Indigo Intuition smoothie, 185

Jícama Un-Fries with Barbecue Dipping Sauce,
    116–18

Kale Caesar, 94–96
Kale Shreds with Cashew Ranch, 178–79
kiwi
    Fruit in Season, 194
    SuperFruit Bowl, 57

mango
    Collard Rollups, 157
    Fruit in Season, 157
    Fruit Smoothie Bowl, 68
    Hardy Harvest, 54
    Mango Pudding, 64
    Zucchini Hummus Wrap, 84–85
Medjool dates
    Almond Milk, 51
    Apple Caramel Tart, 212–13
    Banana Cacao Smoothie, 203
    Banana Vanilla Smoothie, 74
    Cacao Caramel Cupcakes, 206–7
    Carrot-Orange-Lemon Cake, 210–11
    Chia Seed Cranberry Oat Bar, 61
    Coconut Chocolate Truffles, 208
    Detoxifying Green Lemonade, 184
    Indigo Intuition smoothie, 185
    Jícama Un-Fries with Barbecue Dipping Sauce,
        116–18
    Nut Seed and Fruit Bowl, 73
    Quick and Delicious smoothie, 187
    Red High Energy smoothie, 183
    Tropical Paradise with Cashew Cream, 52–53
    Violet Inspiration smoothie, 186
    White Creative smoothie, 187
    Zucchini Ravioli with Sundried Tomato Pesto,
        143–44
mindfulness, 25
Mono Fruit, 69

Naked One-Minute Avocado, 197
Noodle Combo with Asian Sauce, 125–26
Nori sheets, in Friends sof the Nori Roll, 103–4
Nut Butter, Banana, and Veggie Collard Wrap,
    122–23
Nut Butter Green Leaf, 197
Nut Seed and Fruit Bowl, 73

oats
    Chia Seed Cranberry Oat Bar, 61
    Goji Berries and Oats, 76
    Hardy Harvest, 54
Oh So Good Simple Sandwich, 119
Orange Adventure smoothie, 183
organic produce, 29–31
Overstuffed Portobello Mushrooms, 137–38

Pad Thai, 163–65
Parmesan Nut Cheese, 99
peaches
    Fruit in Season, 194
    Orange Adventure smoothie, 183
peanut butter, in Chocolate Almond/Peanut Butter
    Cups, 204
pecans
    Coconut Chocolate Truffles, 208
    Friends of the Nori Roll, 103–4
pestos, 138, 143–44
pineapples
    Fruit in Season, 194
    Fruit Smoothie Bowl, 68
    Tropical Paradise with Cashew Cream, 52
    Yellow Illuminating smoothie, 184
pine nuts
    Overstuffed Portobello Mushrooms, 137–38
    Zucchini Ribbons, 175
Pink Nurturing smoothie, 186
puddings
    Banana Pudding, 77
    Breakfast Pudding, 60
    Chia Pudding, 50
    Chocolate Chia Seed Overnight Pudding, 70
    Chocolate Pudding, 202
    Mango Pudding, 64
pumpkin seeds
    Banana Pudding, 77
    Banana Smoothie Bowl, 66
    Buddha Bowl, 132–33
    Chia Seed Cranberry Oat Bar, 61
    Chocolate Almond/Peanut Butter Cups, 204
    Detox Glow Salad, 86–88
    Fruit Smoothie Bowl, 68
    Hardy Harvest, 54
    Nut Seed and Fruit Bowl, 73
    SuperFruit Bowl, 57

Quick and Delicious smoothie, 187
Quick Granola and Almond Milk, 58

raisins
    Apple Sunrise, 55
    Banana Smoothie Bowl, 66
    Chia Seed Cranberry Oat Bar, 61
    Nut Seed and Fruit Bowl, 73
    Quick Granola and Almond Milk, 58
    Salad in a Jar, 127–29
raspberries, in Red High Energy smoothie, 183
raw diet
    for busy people, 21–24
    lifestyle, 13–15
    motivations, 16–17, 19–21
    origins of, 11
    steps to success, 23
    what to expect, 12–13
Raw Macaroons, 190
Red High Energy smoothie, 183

Salad in a Jar, 127–29
seeds
    . See specific seeds
smoothies, 182–87
soaking, 33
soups
    Creamy Thai Soup, 92–93
    Sweet Corn Chowder, 151
    Vitality Soup, 152–53
    Warm Curried Cream of Carrot Soup, 146
    Warm Noodle Soup, 170
strawberries
    Blue Calming smoothie, 185
    Pink Nurturing smoothie, 186
    Red High Energy smoothie, 183
    Strawberry Banana Ice Cream, 215
Street Taco, 110–11
Stuffed Cremini Mushrooms, 154–55
Stuffed Tomato, 108–9
sundried tomatoes
    Jícama Un-Fries with Barbecue Dipping Sauce, 116–18
    Street Taco, 110
    Stuffed Cremini Mushrooms, 154–55
    Warm Spicy/Mild Chili, 160–61
    Zucchini Ravioli with Sundried Tomato Pesto, 143–44
sunflower seeds
    Banana Almond Butter Sushi, 193
    Banana Pudding, 77
    Banana Smoothie Bowl, 66
    Chia Seed Cranberry Oat Bar, 61
    Chocolate Almond/Peanut Butter Cups, 204
    Detox Glow Salad, 86–88
    Hardy Harvest, 54
    Nut Butter, Banana, and Veggie Collard Wrap, 122–23

Nut Butter Green Leaf, 197
Nut Seed and Fruit Bowl, 73
Quick Granola and Almond Milk, 58
Stuffed Cremini Mushrooms, 154–55
Stuffed Tomato, 108–9
SuperFruit Bowl, 57
Veggie Chop Salad, 173–75
Super Amazing Heirloom Tomato Salad, 82–83
SuperFruit Bowl, 57
Sweet Corn Chowder, 151
Sweet Potato Swirls, 80–81

tahini
    Noodle Combo with Asian Sauce, 125–26
    Warm Noodle Soup, 170–72
    Zucchini Hummus Wrap, 84–85
Tapas Salad, 89–91
Tomato, Cucumber, and Sweet Onion Salad, 166–67
Tomato Veggie Stack, 194
Tri-Colored Sweet Pepper Salad, 115, 145
Tropical Paradise with Cashew Cream, 52–53

vegan diet
    . See raw diet
Vegan Mayonnaise, 109
Veggie Chop Salad, 173–75
Violet Inspiration smoothie, 186
Vitality Soup, 152–53

walnuts
    Apple, Purple Cabbage, and Beet Salad, 120–21
    Cacao Caramel Cupcakes, 206–7
    Carrot-Orange-Lemon Cake, 210–11
    Coconut Chocolate Truffles, 208
    Detox Glow Salad, 86–88
    Filled Sweet Red Bell Pepper, 176–77
    Fresh Fruit Delight, 191
    Goji Berries and Oats, 76
    Overstuffed Portobello Mushrooms, 137
    Quick Granola and Almond Milk, 58
    Street Taco, 110–11
    Tapas Salad, 89–91
    Warm Spicy/Mild Chili, 160–62
Warm Curried Cream of Carrot Soup, 146
Warm Noodle Soup, 170–72
Warm Spicy/Mild Chili, 160–62
White Creative smoothie, 187

Yellow Illuminating smoothie, 184

Zucchini Hummus Wrap, 84–85
Zucchini Ravioli with Sundried Tomato Pesto, 143–44
Zucchini Ribbons, 134
Zucchini Ribbons with Italian Arrabbiata Checca, 158